Contents

Prepared by the staff of

Farm Wife news

Editor: Ann Kaiser
Associate Editor: Cheryl Tevis
Food Editor: Annette Gohlke
Art Director: Keith Bush
Layout and Design: Peggy Bjorkman
Photography: Mike Chiaverina, Keith Bush
Art Associates: Scott Davis, Jan Sanford
Editorial Production: Sally Radtke,
Brenda Gordon
Production Manager: Tom Monday
Publisher: Roy Reiman

733 N. Van Buren
Milwaukee WI 53202
©Farm Wife, Inc., 1976

IF CHRISTMAS—COUNTRY STYLE is what you live and give, this book is especially for you!

The ideas for holiday decorations, gifts and foods in this collection, Another Christmas in the Country, have come directly from the country! They were sent to us by farm and ranch women who have actually made up these decorations and recipes. We've supplemented their ideas with a few of our own as well as a few developed by well-known companies.

If you're like me, as you page through you'll probably make a mental list of which decorations and recipes to try first. And, we'd better get going, 'cause another Christmas in the country is just around the corner!

—Ann Kaiser, Editor

Advent Wreath Is Spiritual Reminder

By Mrs. Frank Miller
Middlebury, Indiana

WE STARTED using an Advent wreath in our home after our first child was born. It is an excellent way to present the Christmas story to a child. We also liked the way it helps us to "prepare our hearts for Christmas".

There are many different variations of the Advent wreath, but they all use four candles arranged around a wreath. One candle is lit for the first Sunday of Advent, which is the fourth Sunday before Christmas. Each Sunday an additional candle is lit—always also lighting the candle or candles from the previous Sundays.

Our family places a red candle in the center of the wreath which is lit on Christmas Eve for Jesus' birthday. The other candles are white. Some people use pink and purple candles.

You may want to purchase a booklet at a religious book store that would give certain scripture readings to go with the lighting of each candle. Or your church may have Advent devotion books available.

Teach your children the symbolization that goes with the wreath so that it has more meaning. For example: *circle formed by wreath = God's eternal love; evergreens = everlasting life; candles = Jesus, the Light of the World; white candles = purity of Christ; red candles = Jesus' shed blood; violet (if that color candles are used) = Jesus is our king and king of repentance.*

One meaning that I found for the individual candles is the following:

first candle = Prophecy Candle
second candle = Bethlehem Candle
third candle = Shepherds' Candle
fourth candle = Angels' Candle

Advent wreaths can be purchased, but there are also inexpensive ways to make them. Here's one idea:

Materials:
Styrofoam wreath form, sprayed green
Wooden base, sprayed green
4 white candles
1 red candle
Artificial holly

Directions:
Using a hand drill, make four evenly spaced holes in Styrofoam to place the four candles. Push plastic holly or evergreens into the wreath to cover Styrofoam. If you choose to use real greens, they would need to be changed several times since the wreath is used for four weeks, and dry greens present a fire hazard.

Untie Bow a Day While Waiting for Christmas

By Mrs. Rodney Voelker
Brownsdale, Minnesota

THE COUNTDOWN to Christmas is always exciting, especially for the children of the household. Here's a perky Santa to help keep track of those exciting December days. It makes a cute door decoration for a child's room, or can brighten your kitchen or family room.

Materials:
Red felt, 24 in. by 3 in.
Felt squares: pink, white, red
2 moveable plastic eyes
24 buttons
24 6-in. pieces green yarn
1 jingle bell
Ribbon bowtie

Directions:
Cut a red felt ribbon 24 in. long by 3 in. wide. Cut Santa's face from felt according to pattern on page 73. Glue head to top of felt ribbon. Glue or sew on ribbon bowtie. Below that sew on jingle bell. Then attach the 24 buttons, spaced evenly, with green yarn pulled through the holes and tied into a bow. Copy the following poem and attach at bottom of felt ribbon below last button. Untie the bottom bow first, beginning December 1, and remove button. (Be sure to save the buttons for next year!)

December the first 'til Christmas
Is the longest time of the year.
Seems as though old Santa
Never will appear!
How many days 'til Christmas?
It's mighty hard to count,
So this little button ribbon
Will tell you the exact amount!
Untie a bow every night
When the Sandman casts his spell,
And Christmas Eve will be here
By the time you reach the bell.

Matchbox Calendar Holds Advent Gifts, Messages

By Karin Belcher
Pollock, Louisiana

WITH CHRISTMAS coming, I would like to share a tradition from my childhood—that of observing the Advent season with a calendar made from matchboxes.

You can decorate the boxes with Christmas motifs cut from old cards, draw them freehand or simply use numbers.

Fill the boxes with pieces of candy, cookies or small toys, reserving something special for the large box for December 24. You may also want to enclose in each box a Bible verse to be read that day.

Materials:
1 yard ribbon, 2 in. wide
23 small matchboxes
1 kitchen matchbox
Glue
Dowel
String
Construction paper or paint

Directions:
Paint tops of matchboxes or cover with construction paper. Apply motifs and/or numbers 1 through 24. Sew a casing at top of ribbon. Slip dowel through and attach string for hanging. Glue matchboxes to ribbon. Fill with goodies.

Candelabra Adds Touch Of Tradition to Season

By Maria Southworth
Lynnwood, Washington

IN BAVARIA, my parents, Georg and Monica Frey, established a tradition of making Christmas candelabras for our relatives during early December. Why not adopt this traditional custom in your family this Christmas season?

Although candelabra decorations can be lavish, you can construct a simple candelabra with some greenery, mistletoe, ribbons and wood.

Materials:
Wooden board, 5-1/2 by 10-1/2 in.
5 pieces of wooden dowel in following lengths: 14-1/2-in., 5-1/2-in., 4-in. and two 3-in.
Short pieces of No. 19 wire
No. 22 spool wire (thin wire)
Slim finishing nails
Red or gold ribbons
Mistletoe
Decorations of your choice

Directions:
Take the 5-1/2-in. piece of dowel and nail it standing upright to the middle of the board. This will be the main stem for the candelabra.

Nail the three short pieces of dowel standing upright on the 14-in. dowel. Place the 4-in. dowel in the middle, with a 3-1/2-in. one on each end. Nail the crossbar to the main stem with finishing nail.

To secure the candles on the upright dowel stems, pound a short piece of heavy No. 19 wire into each dowel and let it stick out about 1/2 in. The stand is now ready to be covered with greenery.

The secret of a smooth and professional-looking candelabra is the tight wrapping of the wire and the even spacing of the branches. The wiring is always done with spool wire in a continuous winding motion, since the branches would not hold together properly if short pieces of wire were used.

Start winding on the left top branch of the candelabra by taking short pieces of fir and carefully fitting them around the short stem. The tips of the branches should face upwards and extend slightly over the tips of the dowel pieces.

Keep wrapping all the way across to the middle branch, then wind the wire (without using branches) around and up to the right top branch.

Proceed, wiring branches around and down in the same manner as for the left side. When the middle part is reached again, wrap the wire again upwards to the middle branch and then finish off by wrapping the branches all the way down to the board. Small imperfections at the joining crosses can be easily hidden by placing a ribbon or decoration over the spot.

After the main stem is completely covered, wind the wire around the stem a couple more times and then cut it off. Tuck the ends securely between the branches.

To cover the flat board, insert branches long enough in proportion to the whole design underneath the wires. If the wire has been tightened enough, the branches will hold securely. Should there be some doubt as to the stability of the whole arrangement, a couple of small nails can be pounded into the thicker ends of the branches and into the board.

Now decorate. Ribbon tufts can be made by forming three loops and tying them together with thin wire. Insert tufts on each of the outside branches, using a slightly larger one at the base of the main stem.

A couple of cones or heavier decorations should be inserted at the base and the smaller decorations placed at the top.

To finish, tie the mistletoe to the base of the main stem, then force three candles down over the heavy wire stems at the top of the three branches.

To make a candelabra with only one main stem, start wrapping from the top down, then wind a piece of ribbon around the stem and perhaps across the flat board. The decorations should be kept smaller and a little less elaborate than for the larger 3-branch candelabra.

Dress Up Windows For the Holidays

By Mrs. Jim Torrance
Good Hope, Illinois

MAKE your window to the world a festive sight this Holiday Season with a roll of red tape, a can of spray snow and a string of Christmas tree lights.

Materials:
Red tape
Spray snow
Christmas lights

Directions:
Divide each half of the window into fourths, using red tape to mark divisions. Then, spray each window pane with spray snow around outer edges only.

String Christmas tree lights around outside of the window outdoors and let window frame your Christmas tree inside your home.

Straw Star Tells Advent Meaning

By Mrs. Otto Fahning
Wells, Minnesota

THE ADVENT star shown here is created by using a 6-pointed straw star and a 2-fold straw star in the center, decorated with evergreen and purple, color of Advent. You can obtain the straw from a farmer, florist or craft shop.

Materials:
Straw
   36 18-in. lengths
    4 5-in. lengths
    4 2-1/2-in. lengths
Beige heavy-duty sewing thread
Purple embroidery floss
3 purple chenille stems
10-in. wire
Sprigs of Japanese yew

Directions:

Let straw lengths soak in water for several hours. A plate may be put on top of the straw to keep it submerged. If the straw becomes dry while you're working with it, wet it again.

Sort 18-in. lengths into six groups of six straws. Make one triangle using three groups of six, tying ends together with thread.

Weave the three remaining groups over and under straws of first triangle and tie ends together to form second triangle. Tie also at the places where the triangles intersect.

Cut each chenille strip into four pieces and cover thread with it. Twist chenille wire to hold at back of star.

The 2-fold star in the center of the larger star is made from two Simple Stars. Here's how to make them: Place two of the 5-in. straws together to form a cross and the other two to form an "X" and put one on top of the other. Bind the star with purple floss alternating over one straw and under the next, remembering the thread is always brought over the straws that lie on top and under the straws that lie at the bottom. Repeat with the four 2-1/2-in. lengths.

Join the two simple stars by placing the smaller on top of the larger and binding with floss.

Cover a 10-in. length of wire with Japanese yew sprigs and attach star (see photo). Then fasten 2-fold star at center of greenery.

You can hang your Advent star on a solid-colored wall or door, or you may want to mount it on a background of colored paper or fabric for greater contrast.

It's Christmas!

At last it is December
And the air is silver-sheer.
Bright messages are coming
From folks both far and near.

There is evidence of secrets
In the closet, in the chest.
And the children, though it's trying,
Are behaving at their best.

There are pies stacked in the freezer—
Pumpkin, mince and apple too;
Plus a note tacked to the cupboard:
"Christmas Eve, make oyster stew."

Brother's practicing a reading.
Grandma's humming "Silent Night."
And the angel's in a dither,
For her wings don't look quite right.

Now the tree's up in one corner,
Fragrant pine boughs flank the door.
And the house is decorated
From the ceiling to the floor.

Candle flames begin to flicker,
Distant bells begin to peal.
Suddenly there is a silence—
Lowly subjects pause to kneel.

Everything is Christmas-ready,
Hearts and homes are filled with love.
All because there is a manger
Lighted by a star above.

—Faye Tanner Cool
Fleming, Colorado

Make a "Greeting Banner" This Year

Your church group or club members can extend Christmas greetings to each other on this attractive felt banner. Then use the money saved on cards and postage for a special contribution or project.

By Lynn Wahner
Milwaukee, Wisconsin

YOU CAN send Christmas greetings to all the members of your church, club or women's organization, using a Christmas card banner like this one. It's a thoughtful idea and can also be an enjoyable way to raise money for the church or group.

Each member who wants to send Christmas wishes to the group puts her name on a paper "ornament" which is used to decorate the tree on the banner. Money that would normally be spent for cards and postage can be contributed to the organization instead.

Place the finished banner just inside in a convenient location in your church or meeting hall. Cut paper ornaments in the shape of bells, wreaths, balls, stars, and so on. Set up a table for the ornaments, red and green felt tip pens and a box for contributions. Members can fill out their own ornaments and place them on the tree. If you are not using adhesive-backed paper, supply masking tape to attach the ornaments to the tree.

Directions for the banner, given below, can be modified in size according to the number of people who will be using the banner.

Materials:
3 yds. red felt, 36 in. wide
1-1/2 yds. green felt, 36 in. wide
10 yds. metallic gold rick-rack
1 yd. gold fringe
1-1/4 yd. heavy gold cord
Curtain rod or heavy dowel, about 38 in. long

Directions:
Draw a Christmas tree, freehand, about 1 yd. wide at its base and 1-1/2 yd. high. Cut this pattern from the green felt. Fold the red felt in half and glue the tree to one side of the red felt, with the base of the tree trunk centered on the cut edge of the felt.

Sew the two layers of red felt together about 2 in. from the fold. The double thickness of felt gives the banner more weight and allows it to hang better. Cut a strip of green felt 5 in. wide and 36 in. long. Place this over the fold in the banner and stitch through both layers of red and green felt. Slip the curtain rod or dowel between the layers.

Outline the branches of the tree in gold rick-rack, gluing it to the felt. Cut two pieces of rick-rack 36 in. long. Intertwine the two pieces for a braided look and sew the braided rick-rack in place along the edge of the green border at the top of the banner.

Sew the gold fringe across the bottom of the banner, sewing through one or both layers of red felt. Tie the gold cord to each end of the rod. Your banner can be hung on a banner stand or on the wall.

Handmade Cards and Notes Personalize Your Greeting

By Marie Olsen
Heartwell, Nebraska

WHO HAS a well-filled purse at Holiday time? Just the annual exchange of season's greetings with friends and relatives can really put a dent in anyone's budget.

How about making your own Christmas cards this year, thus saving their purchase price to buy the stamps you need?

Also you can make plain stationery holiday-special and use it for all your letters and notes this Christmas season.

There are many, many designs to use on handmade cards and on the corners of stationery. Here are just a few:

Poinsettias: Cut 8 petals of tissue paper, use mustard seeds for the center, draw leaves and stem with green pen.

Candle and Bible: Cut narrow red rick-rack candle, use purchased Bible sticker, draw evergreen limbs with green pen, put two small tats at base of candle.

Honeycomb wreath and tree: Cut shapes from green honeycomb ribbon, trim with foil paper punch-outs, star for tree top, bow for wreath.

Pinecone: Draw brown pinecone and green evergreen limbs with marking pens, use silver glitter nail polish over cone for sparkly effect.

Candy canes: Cut canes from white paper and draw red lines with marking pen. Use two canes back to back and trim with holly leaves and berries cut from foil paper.

Christmas stocking: Cut from red and white felt, top with holly and berries.

Snowman: Trace two circles the size of a quarter, draw hat and features with pen. Cover with glitter or glittery nail polish.

Remember, colored pens, pencils, chalk, nail polish (colored and glittered), paper punches, stickers, etc. all help add to the fun!

The Holidays — Heavenly or Hectic?

By Shirley A. Harvey
Barre, Vermont

HOW ARE the holidays at your house—a happy, relaxed time with the house attractively decorated and everything polished to gleaming perfection; delicious food and snacks ready for guests who drop in; and all the shopping, mailing and wrapping done early? Or does Christmas Eve find you frantically stuffing the stockings and the turkey, vacuuming glitter off the rug, writing the last cards and wondering what to feed the Wilsons who've called to say they're coming over?

Most of us fall somewhere in between, and each year we resolve to be more organized—to get things done early so we can keep some of the holiday spirit and not be too exhausted to enjoy this very special time of year.

Of course, no one can plan someone else's holiday. Each family has its own traditions and favorite foods and fun—things that are so much a part of them that any changes would spoil Christmas. But often planning or simplification or even changing your way of thinking can ease the work and make your holidays more rewarding. Here are a few ideas that may help:

Make your holidays really yours— Stop and evaluate. Are you doing some things just from habit that take time and energy and don't really add that much enjoyment? For instance, are you doing something all the neighbors do, but that your family doesn't care about one way or another? That's a good thing to drop from *your* Christmas.

Do you still stencil the windows because your youngsters enjoyed it? Maybe they've outgrown Santa and his reindeer on the windowpanes—so why go to all the extra work.

Do everything you can ahead— The after-holiday sales are a wonderful time to pick up cards, paper, decorations and even gifts for next year; and an added bonus is that the stores aren't crowded and you save money! Do your cleaning ahead so that during the last few busy days you can "skim over the top".

Prepare as much of your holiday food in advance as you possibly can. In addition to cookies and candy, you can double recipes for casseroles, spaghetti, stews, etc., and freeze half— what a help to have a pot of delicious beef stew ready for the night you finish your shopping, and you feel like dropping! Pies and breads can all be made ahead and frozen, too.

Stay within your budget . . . almost —This may not sound like a way to make your holidays less hectic, but it is. Spending a lot more than you can afford can create tension and spoil the whole feeling of Christmas! Don't worry if some people give you more costly gifts than you gave them—price shouldn't be the measure of a gift.

Select your gifts with your head as well as your heart. Keep your ears and eyes open through the year and you'll know that elderly Mr. Brown down the street would enjoy a box of homemade sugar cookies more than another necktie to lay away in his top drawer.

And you'll give Aunt Julie a subscription to her favorite magazine because it will help her pass the long evenings, instead of sending her the usual pastel cardigan. Or how about a personal note or phone call rather than a gift for someone who "has everything".

Make time for what's really important— For going to church with the whole family, for reading the beautiful Christmas story from the Bible, for singing a few carols, for *being together.*

Find time to contact sick or lonely people. A nice way to do this is to put the names of a few who need a little special cheer into a hat and let each family member draw one out; and then sometime during the holidays do something for them—a call, note or small gift. This takes some of the burden off Mom and also teaches sharing and compassion.

Be sure to make time to help younger members of the family with costumes, parts in programs etc., and *go to the programs your children are in!* A youth choir singing the beautiful songs of Christmas can touch your heart as no other part of the holidays can.

Enlist all the help you can— a family trimming the tree together is a Christmas tradition, but how about teenagers helping wrap gifts, going to the post office or doing other errands. Boys can put up outside lights and decorations; girls can enjoy and learn by helping with the baking, even a toddler can cut out cookies. This can make everything more meaningful for the whole family. Get Dad to write notes to go in some of the Christmas cards—especially to *his* relatives!

Plan to enjoy the holidays— You can get so busy doing everything else that you leave out something very important—enjoying yourself. Somehow plan time to relax and rest, have your hair done, buy or make a new dress—or whatever will add that extra sparkle. A lot of the shine is taken away from Christmas if Mom is tired and cross.

Don't get upset— This is so important! Realize that there's going to be a last minute rush, a few unexpected guests, and that one of the kids will inform you (as you tuck him into bed at night) that he needs 3 dozen cookies to take to school in the morning for the Christmas party! This is all part of Christmas and—if you keep the right perspective—part of the fun!

These hints may not make your holidays completely heavenly; but they can make them a little less hectic. We need the lift and the inspiration that Christmas can bring and if "Peace on Earth" can be in one small corner of the world—our homes—that's a beginning.

"Night Before Christmas" Sleigh Scene

By Marla Fattig
Brady, Nebraska

"WHAT TO MY wondering eyes should appear than this miniature sleigh and eight tiny reindeer!" You can make this vision a *reality*. With just a few yards of dotted swiss or gingham material, some felt, ribbon and rick-rack, you can create a reindeer and sleigh scene for your own home.

Materials:

1/4 yd. brown print fabric
1/4 yd. coordinating brown print fabric (dotted swiss and gingham work well)
1/4 yd. white cotton fabric
Stuffing
Crochet hook
Black embroidery floss
4 white and 4 brown small fringe balls
11 by 11-in. square brown felt
11 by 11-in. square white felt
1 pkg. Coats & Clark's Polyweb
1-1/2 yd. ribbon braid
3 yd. coordinating medium rick-rack
10 by 15-in. thin white cardboard
White paper, striped with brown marker
Glue

1-1/4 yd. cord

Directions for Reindeer:

Using patterns on pages 75-79, add 1/4-in. seam allowance to pattern for upper body and underbody. Cut eight white underbodies and mark darts. Fold legs up on fold lines and stitch darts. Clip. Cut eight checked and eight dotted upper body pieces. With right sides together, baste two matching body pieces together from mark at neck, around top to mark at rear. Stitch; clip seam carefully.

Baste underbody to upper body, leaving open at rear to turn and stuff. Stitch; clip seam. Turn right side out, using a crochet hook. Stuff firmly, again using crochet hook. Slipstitch opening. Embroider eyes with floss. To make tails, sew brown balls to four of reindeer and white balls to other four reindeer.

Ears: Cut four ears of one fabric and four of other fabric. Leaving a small opening for turning, stitch the two layers together around ear shapes. Turn right side out, and slipstitch opening. Pinch fabric together in middle to form two ears from each ear piece. Tack to top of head.

Antlers: Cut felt pieces in half. Using Polyweb, fuse together two layers brown and two layers white. Cut four brown and four white antlers, fold each in half. Position long horns in back and tack to head in front of ears.

Trim: Cut braid into eight 6-in. lengths. Stitch rick-rack to edges and wrap the braid around deer, tacking under the body.

Directions for Sleigh:

Trace sleigh patterns on cardboard. Cut out. Run a knife lightly along fold lines. Using paper you "striped" brown, cut out side, back, and front panels. Glue in place on sleigh. Fold sleigh to shape and glue flaps on inside.

Trace runner patterns onto cardboard and cut out. Design can be cut out or drawn. Score fold lines. Fold and glue to shape. Glue to base of sleigh.

Join reindeer by running cord through braid trim on bodies. Wrap tiny boxes with assorted print fabrics and place them in sleigh. I have added a Santa which was made from a round tree ornament.

Made of pop cans covered with quilt batting . . .

Carolers Sing Out Christmas

By Nancy Myers
Olney, Illinois

NO CHRISTMAS SEASON is complete without carolers. But, you don't have to wait until they come to your door—you can make a cherubic pair like this one from pop cans, quilt batting and a few other simple materials.

Materials:
Two 12-oz. pop cans
Two 3-in. Styrofoam balls
White dacron quilt batting
Felt: red, black, green
Colored sequins
2 pipe cleaners

Directions:

Cut the bottom entirely out of the cans and make a 1-1/2-in. hole in the tops. This hole can be made with small tin snips or by placing the can over a solid object and cutting the top with a chisel and hammer. You may wish to wrap the outside of the cans in a piece of tissue paper to protect the dacron from the rough edges of the can.

Next, spread the dacron quilt batting to a single thickness. Cut two pieces 11 by 18-in. and wrap one piece around each can. Glue the edges down. Cut two 11-in. squares. Wrap each Styrofoam ball in a square, smoothing down the wrinkles as much as possible —this is the head.

Fasten the dacron around the head with a pipe cleaner. Put your hand carefully up into the can and pull the dacron tails on the ball-head into the 1-1/2-in. hole in the top of the can, pulling the top edges of the dacron wrapped around the can into the hole as well. Push the dacron at the bottom of the can into the can. Now you have the head and body.

Cut two pieces of dacron 4-1/2 by 15 in. for the arms. Fold each side lengthwise to the center, and staple or pin the end edges together.

Cut two pieces of dacron 6 by 6-1/2 in. for the muffs. Fold the edges of the muffs to the center and staple or pin the muff over the joining ends of the arms. Place the arms over the head and around the can. The arms should be at the top of the can in the back and extend halfway or more down the front, with the muff below the face.

Cut two pieces 11 by 12 in. for the hats. Fold the pieces together to form a tube and staple or pin the lapped edges. Fold up a 2-in. brim on the hats. Fold the lady's hat in at the top and staple or pin shut.

For the man's hat, take a needle and thread and make a topknot about 2 in. from the top. Pull the thread tight and fasten. Place hats on the heads. Use red, green and black felt to cut out the pieces below for the faces and trim. I trim the lady's hat and muff with colored sequins. Place the carolers on a board or wooden shingle, decorate with greenery, and you have a lovely table decoration.

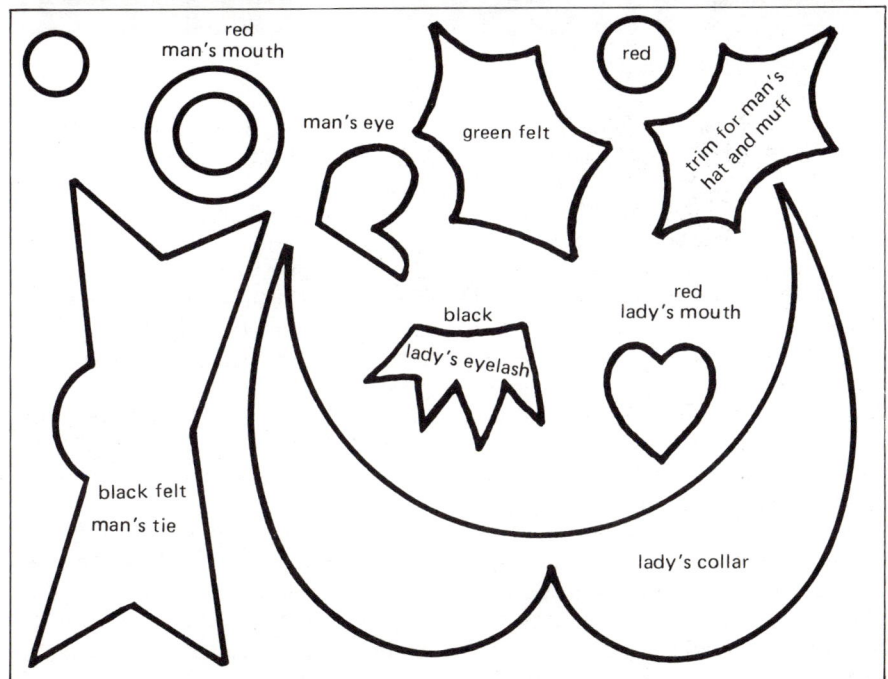

red
man's mouth

man's eye

red

trim for man's hat and muff

green felt

black
lady's eyelash

red
lady's mouth

black felt
man's tie

lady's collar

These cheery "Milk Can Kids", shown in color on the cover, make a unique outdoor decoration for your farm home during the holidays.

Milk Can Kids Greet Guests and Passersby

By Peggy Bjorkman
Farm Wife News Illustrator

THE IDEA for the "Milk Can Kids" shown on these pages and on the cover of this book came to me on my way back from my folks' farm in northern Wisconsin.

The staff of *Another Christmas in the Country* had been thinking of ways to say "Merry Christmas", country style. I thought of Dad's old milk cans, Mom's tubes of paint and my brothers' and sisters' old hats.

As I passed through one rural community, I noticed their fire hydrants painted up to look like little people. With that, I put all these thoughts together to get—Milk Can Kids!

So, look around for a couple of milk cans. If you have some left-over acrylic paints, use those. Otherwise you can purchase paints.

You can adapt this idea to your own color preferences or make the clothes a color like someone's in your family. The same goes for the hair and eyes. Make the kids personal.

An old stretched-out hat can be used for the topping off. I was lucky to find hats to match my color scheme. You might want to pick the hat, then coordinate the colors around it.

Place your Milk Can Kids in the front yard or by your driveway—wherever guests or passersby will see their cheery faces! Have fun with this unique way to say "Merry Christmas" —country style!

Materials:
2 milk cans (I used 10-gal.)
2 8-in. Styrofoam balls
1 small can flesh-colored spray paint (make sure label says it can be used on Styrofoam)
Acrylic paints: red, yellow, blue, green, black, white, brown
Paint brushes, 1-in. and 3/8-in.
Glue
2 hats
2 scarves

Directions:
Make sure surface of cans is clean.

Boy: Using the larger brush, paint top of can and lid red. Paint handles red and continue on down to below rim of milk can with red. (It may take two or three layers of paint to make it

Paint hairline. Fill in with brown. Hairline on girl looks like this:

Paint on hairline and fill in with yellow.

It's fun to make their faces. I made their eyes looking toward each other. The smiles and the noses are simple lines. Take your time. Go slowly. The Styrofoam texture is a little rough, so it may take going over with your small brush a few times.

Let everything dry.

Glue heads to centers of lids. Let dry. Put on hats and scarves.

Above, you see how the "kids" look from the back. Note how the boy's jean straps cross. At right is a close-up view of the boy's face and neck to show the detail.

even, depending on the surface of your can. If you start with a painted can, I'd suggest you give the whole thing a base coat of white. That will make the colors look brighter.)

Paint the bottom of the can blue. Paint thin lines for straps. Fill in with blue. (Use masking tape to get the lines straight.)

Using the smaller brush, outline straps of blue jeans in white. Carefully paint white lines for buckles. See photo for how straps cross in the back.

Girl: With larger brush, paint top half of can and entire lid green, and bottom half of can red. Paint on black belt and buttons. With smaller brush, paint white outline between belt, belt buckles and holes.

Heads: Take a sharp knife and cut bottom of Styrofoam balls so they will rest flat on top of milk cans. Spray with flesh-colored paint. Lightly draw in features. If you want to practice, paint face on where hair will be. Then you can just paint hair over your practice face. Hairline on boy looks like this:

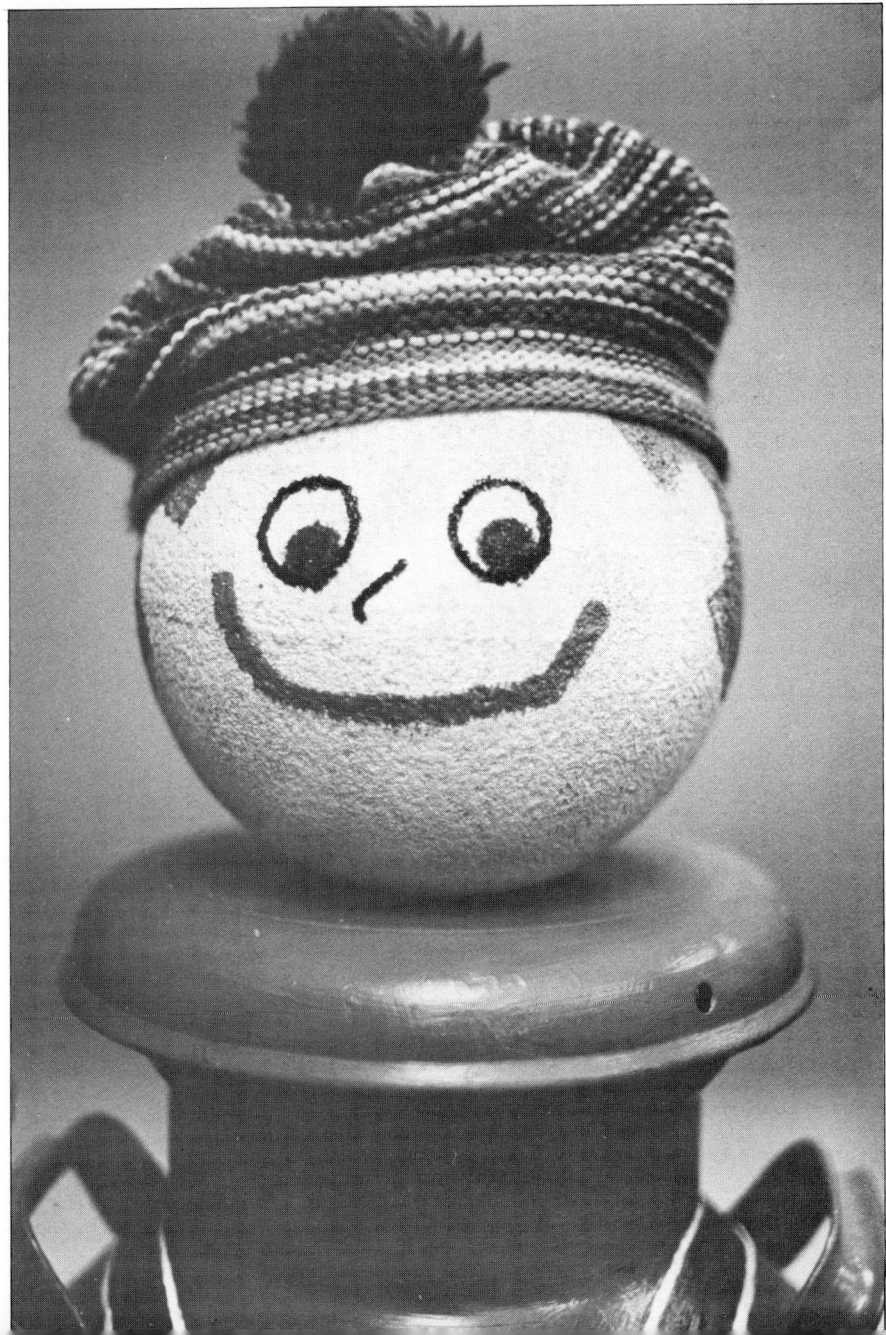

"Santa's Swingers" Made of Spools

By June Rose Mobly
New Matamoras, Ohio

"SANTA'S SWINGERS" form a colorful little Christmas scene made almost entirely from empty thread spools.

Construction of the 11 spool figures is simple. And, they form a lively, joyful and amusing group when arranged as shown in the photo below.

REINDEER (9)

Materials:
9 spools, approx. 1-7/16 in.
   across top
9 Styrofoam balls, 1-1/8-in. diameter
Glue
Light cardboard
Felt scraps: red, blue, black, white
9 white pipe cleaners
Poster paints; brown, yellow, blue, red,
   green, white, orange, black

Directions:

All nine reindeer are made the same way. The only difference is that eight of them have a black nose and one (Rudolph) has a red nose.

Paint spools brown. Glue a Styrofoam ball to one end of each spool. Cut eyes of blue felt, nose of black felt (one of red), mouth of red felt and hooves of white felt. (You may use colored paper instead of felt, if you prefer.) Glue to head and body.

Glue a pipe cleaner around the top of each spool for arms. Dot the pipe cleaner with brown poster paint.

Cut antlers, tails and musical instruments from light cardboard, following patterns below. Paint with poster paints in the indicated colors and glue onto reindeer.

To give the effect of "dancing" reindeer, glue pieces of heavy cardboard to the bottoms of the spools so the reindeer will be tilted in various ways: forward, sideways, backward.

SANTA

Materials:
1 spool, approx. 1-7/16 in. across top
Red poster paint
1 Styrofoam ball,
approx. 1-1/8 in. diameter
Felt scraps: red, white, blue, black
Glue
1 white pipe cleaner

Directions:

Paint spool red. Glue Styrofoam ball to one end of spool for head. Cut Santa's cap, face, beard, belt, boots and mittens according to patterns and colors indicated below and glue to head and body. Glue on pipe cleaner for arms and glue mitten to ends of pipe cleaner.

CHRISTMAS TREE

Materials:
4 spools: approx. 1-7/16 in.,
   1-1/8 in., 15/16 in., 7/8 in.
Glue
Poster paints: green, yellow, blue,
   red, white
Felt scraps: red, white
Cardboard

Directions:

Use second-smallest spool (15/16 in.) for base of tree. Paint it yellow

and blue. Paint other three spools green. Glue green spools together to form tree, with largest spool at the bottom. Glue tree to base.

Decorate tree with ornaments cut from red and white felt. Cut star from cardboard and paint according to pattern below. Insert star stem into hole of top spool.

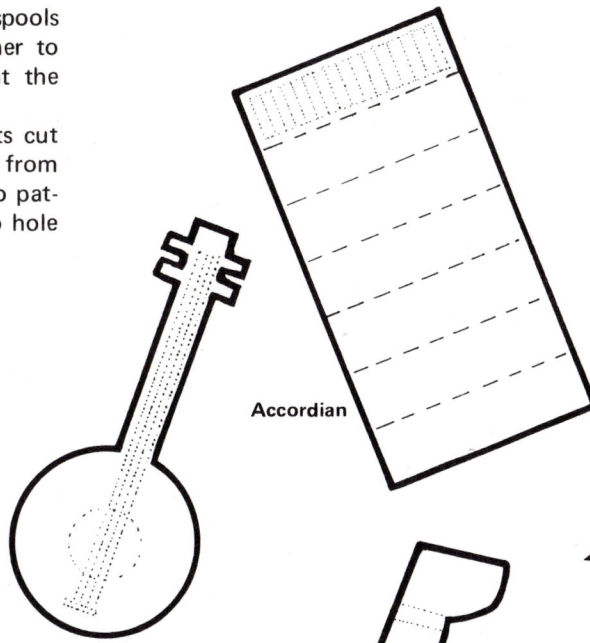

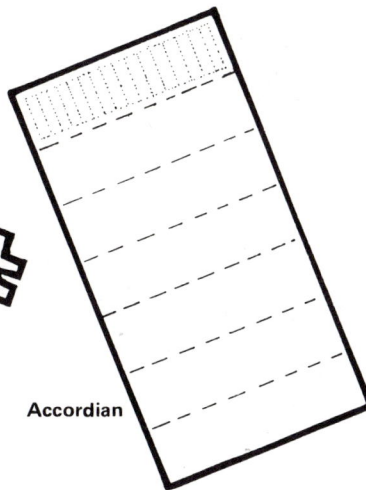

Accordian

Banjo

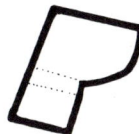

Santa's Foot

Star for Tree

Santa's Beard

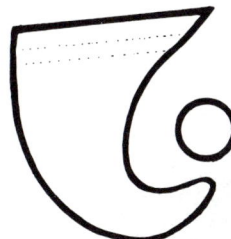

Santa's Hat

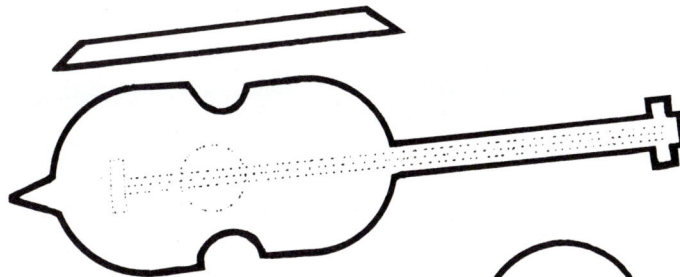

Cello

Tail

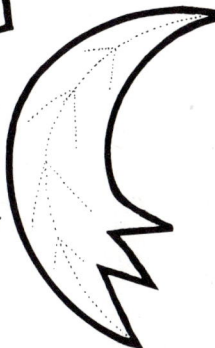

Antler

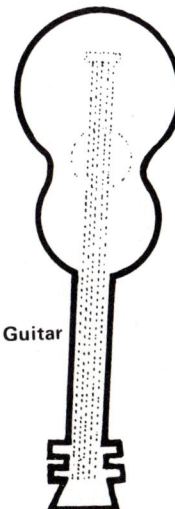

Guitar

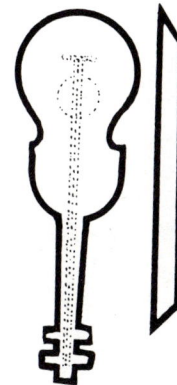

Violin

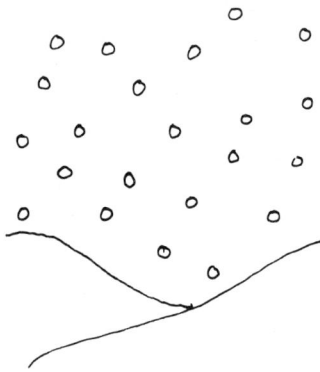

Tiny Snowman Is Big on Spirit

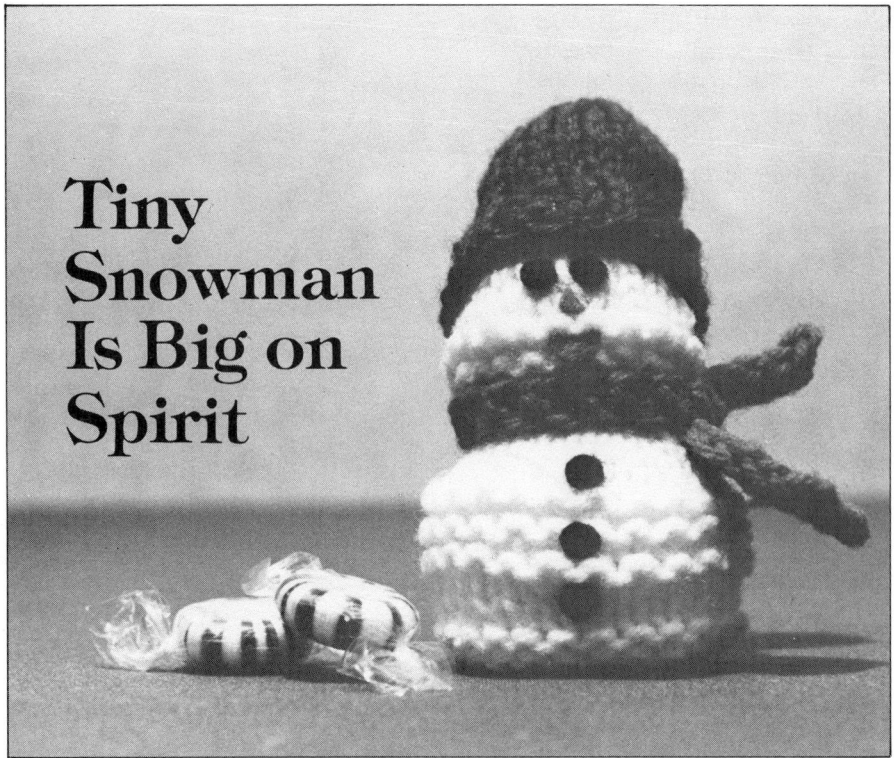

This cute snowman can be knit up quickly and used as a table favor or small gift. If you make several, you may want to vary the color of the hats and scarves.

By Nancy Joens
Hopkins, Minnesota

THIS cute knit snowman can be used to decorate your tree, as a table favor or in a centerpiece. If you wish to make him larger, use larger Styrofoam balls and increase pattern accordingly.

Materials:
White and red (or green) 4-ply yarn
No. 5 knitting needles
2 Styrofoam balls, 1-1/2 and 2 in.
Red and black felt scraps

Directions:
Gauge: 5 sts per inch.
Snowman: With white yarn, cast on 26 sts. Rows 1-3: Garter stitch (knit every row). Rows 4-6: Stockinette stitch (knit and purl alternating rows). Rows 7-12: Garter stitch. Rows 13-15: Stockinette stitch. Rows 16-22: Garter stitch. Rows 23-25: Stockinette stitch. Rows 26-27: Garter stitch. Rows 27-28: Knit, decreasing 4 sts each row (18 sts).

Break yarn leaving 12-in. end. Draw end through remaining sts, draw up tightly and fasten off. Sew side seam.

Slide the 1-1/2-in. ball into drawn-up end for head. Cut a small amount of Styrofoam off the 2-in. ball so it will stand. Place in "body" end of snowman.

Glue or tack on two black felt circles for eyes, 3 black circles for buttons, red triangle nose and red moon mouth.

Stocking Cap: With red or green yarn, cast on 24 sts. Work in K2, P2 ribbing for 4 rows. Work stockinette stitch until piece measures 2 in., ending with purl row. K2 tog across next row. Purl one row. K2 tog across (6 sts). Break yarn leaving 12-in. end. Finish as for snowman.

Scarf: With red or green yarn, cast on 6 sts. Row 1-6: Garter stitch. Row 7: K1, K2 tog, K1 (4 sts). Row 8: Knit. Row 9: K1, K2 tog, K1 (3 sts). Work these 3 sts in garter stitch for 7-1/2 in. Next row (1): K1, inc 1 in next st, K1 (4 sts). Row 2: Knit. Row 3: K1, inc 1 in each of next 2 sts, K1 (6 sts). Row 4: Bind off as if to knit, work end into edge.

Bowling Pin Santa And Mrs. Could Be Right Up Your Alley

By Ann Kaiser
Brookfield, Wisconsin

DO YOU recognize the shapes of this Christmas couple? If you guessed bowling pins, you're right! Santa and Mrs. Claus are knit and decorated, then slipped over old bowling pins.

Check with your local bowling alley for pins that have cracked or split. The alleys usually give away the damaged pins or charge only a small amount.

Mr. and Mrs. Claus will surely draw compliments as they welcome guests to your home this Christmas.

Materials:

Knitting needles, No. 7 and No. 9
4 oz. worsted weight red yarn
2 oz. worsted weight pink yarn
2 oz. worsted weight white yarn
4 movable eyes
12 in. black braid
3 black buttons
Gold or silver wire
Red and black felt scraps
Glue

Directions for Santa:

With red yarn and No. 7 needles, cast on 50 sts. Rib (K1, P1) for five rows.

Change to No. 9 needles and work stockinette stitch (K one row, P one row) for 30 rows.

On next 24 rows, decrease 4 sts evenly every 3 rows (28 sts remain).

Change to No. 7 needles and rib 5 rows. Change to pink yarn and rib 5 more rows. With pink yarn and No. 9 needles, work in stockinette stitch 20 rows.

Decrease one st at each end of every row for next 6 rows (16 sts). K2 tog across next two knit rows (4 sts remain). Run yarn through remaining 4 sts and draw together.

Clock. Sew seam; pull Santa down around bowling pin. Glue on movable eyes. Cut eyebrows, nose and mouth of felt and glue on. Loop white yarn for beard and sew on. Sew or glue on black braid for belt and black buttons.

Stocking Hat: With white yarn and No. 7 needles, cast on 44 sts and rib for 5 rows. Change to No. 9 needles and red yarn. Work in stockinette stitch decreasing one st at each end of every knit row until 2 sts remain. Fasten off. Block hat. Sew seam. Make small white yarn pom-pom and sew to tip of hat.

Directions for Mrs. Claus:

With white yarn and No. 9 needles, cast on 110 sts. Work garter stitch (K every row) for 8 rows. Change to red yarn and work stockinette stitch for 60 rows.

Knit 2 tog across next row (55 sts remain). Purl back. Decrease 17 sts in next row (28 sts remain). Purl back. Decrease 17 sts in next row (28 sts remain). Purl back.

Change to No. 7 needles and pink yarn; rib 5 rows. Finish head section as for Santa.

Glue on movable eyes. Cut eyebrows, nose and mouth of felt and glue on. Make small white pom-poms for front of dress. Bend wire to form glasses and stitch ear pieces to sides of head.

To make hair, wrap white yarn carefully around an 8-in. piece of cardboard about 40 times. Holding yarn at one end of the cardboard, cut strands at other end. Sew down middle of hair strands on machine to form the part. Sew hair onto head. Tie ends together and tuck under into a bun at nape of neck. If you'd like, add a crocheted dusting cap.

Collar: With No. 7 needles and white yarn, cast on 45 sts and work in garter stitch for 7 rows. Bind off.

Daisy Snowman Decorates Your Home for Holidays

By Mrs. Don Mazour
Lawrence, Nebraska

YOU DON'T have to wait until it snows to build your own snowman! With a little Styrofoam, Swisstraw, felt and ribbon, you can have a snowman centerpiece this Christmas season.

Materials:
2 Styrofoam balls
    (4 to 5 in. in diameter)
Daisy loom
Swisstraw
Straight pins
Red or black felt
Ribbon
Construction paper

Directions:

Remove just a sliver of each Styrofoam ball, so that balls will glue together smoothly. Remove a sliver from bottom of large ball and glue to round, flat Styrofoam base.

Using a daisy loom, make as many small daisies as needed to cover the balls. Attach daisies with straight pins, placing two daisy centers as eyes, one for nose, three for mouth and three on the larger ball to form buttons.

Cut a piece of red or black felt to fit the center for the eyes, nose, mouth and buttons. Tie a ribbon around snowman's neck and make a hat out of construction paper. Decorate base with ribbon.

CHRISTMAS PERSONALITIES

18

Put Your Little Angels to Work

By Maria Southworth
Lynnwood, Washington

CHRISTMAS IS a time of joy and laughter for children and for all the young at heart. For a last-minute craft project, children can make a lovely angel either as a gift or a decoration in your home. Encircle the angel with Christmas greenery for a centerpiece or make a smaller version and attach a string hanger for hanging on the Christmas tree.

Materials:
1-1/2-in. satin-covered Styrofoam ball
Cardboard for cone
Remnant material, such as satin,
    brocade or taffeta
Gold decorative foil
1/2 yd. gold braid, 1-in. wide
1/2 yd. narrow braid
Curly angel hair
Tacky glue

Directions:
Make cardboard cone by gluing ends of cone together. Cut material for dress, using the cone pattern. Spread glue around edges of cone, and glue dress material to it.

Affix Styrofoam head to top of cone with glue, then arrange curly angel hair on top of head and around sides. Use only a very small amount of glue to hold hair in place. Glue braid around neck to hide any imperfection.

Cut foil arms and wings according to pattern. Glue arms to the back of cone, about halfway down the middle.

Cut two pieces of 1-in. wide gold braid, each 5 in. long. Fold each piece in half, then loop them over the arms of angel for sleeves. A dab of glue close to front of arms will secure sleeve braid to body.

Affix wings to back, making sure bottom part of both wings are at even heights.

Bend wings slightly backwards at tips and at sides.

Glue narrow braid around bottom of skirt, then place a 3-in. piece of braid between curly hair for a halo.

Hurricane Santa Holds Holiday Goodies

IF YOU'D like a special container for your Christmas candy and a cute centerpiece for the holidays, you'll have both with this clever hurricane Santa.

Fill him with peppermints, foil-wrapped chocolate ornaments or the candy of your choice. If you want to see the candy disappear fast, just tell your family to pull off Santa's hat to get at the goodies.

Materials:
Glass lamp chimney,
    approx. 8-1/2 in. high
Red corduroy
Felt: white, red, black
9 in. green satin ribbon
Jingle bell
Glue
Styrofoam to fit chimney bottom

Directions:
Cut Santa's face from felt according to pattern on page 83. Glue on to glass chimney. Cut a Styrofoam plug for bottom of chimney to form base. Cut hat pattern from corduroy and felt. With right sides together, sew along curved edges of hat. Turn. Glue or sew on white trim.

Sew bell to top of hat. Tie bow of green ribbon around base of bell. Fill Santa with candy.

Trim Your Tree With Needlepoint

By Mae Bierman
Hartland, Wisconsin

WHEN it comes to needlepoint, Christmas offers so many possibilities for designs! I try to come up with some new ones each year which can be used as decorations and tree ornaments.

They make delightful gifts and really sell at fairs and bazaars. I left our church Harvest Festival last year with all the items I'd made up sold and orders for many more—to be finished and delivered before Christmas!

Here are some of my favorite designs. I think you'll enjoy making them and hope they'll be some of your treasured holiday decorations for years to come.

General Directions:

Cut the canvas in a straight line between the mesh. Allow 1-in. margin on sides of design. Bind the canvas edges with masking tape.

Lay canvas over patterns on pages 00-00. Use Sanford's Nepo needlework markers or paint with acrylic paint.

Work design using two threads of Persian yarn. Note: One strand of yarn is three threads. Length is usually 30 in. or buy 1 yd. for one strand.

To block: Put needlepoint face down on several thicknesses of towel, cover with pressing cloth, press with steam iron set on steam-wood. Pull opposite corners to square up the canvas and press. Repeat pulling and pressing until sides are square. Let dry thoroughly. Canvas will become stiff again.

To finish: Cut around worked design about 1/2 in. from work. Cut on straight of mesh between threads. Be-fore turning canvas to back to work, clip at intervals nearly to stitches. Catch-stitch edges to back of work and press again. If there are buttons, sequins or other trims, attach now. Attach elastic cord for hanging.

Using pattern, cut a piece of felt for backing. Cut two pieces of polyester quilt batting for stuffing. Place batting on back side, place felt backing over batting and sew together with overcast stitch.

THESE ORIGINAL Christmas needlepoint designs will be treasured by your family and friends. Opposite page shows freestanding Angel. At left are Candy Cane, Bargello Stockings, French Boot. Above are Santa in His House and Rocking Horse. And below, The Three Bears.

BARGELLO STOCKINGS (Easy)

Materials:
14-mesh or 16-mesh canvas, 5-in. by
    6-in. (full strand on 14; two
    threads on 16)
12 strands Persian yarn
1/4 yd. velvet ribbon
Size 20 tapestry needle
1 square felt

Directions:
Using pattern on page 86, work stocking in Bargello stitch of your choice in two or three colors. If you wish, work heel and toe in kalem or reverse tent stitch. Follow general directions for marking and finishing. Cut two pieces of felt from pattern. Attach ribbon hanger on back after turning back edges. Sew one piece of felt along top of stocking, lay on other piece and overcast stitch both layers around stocking.

THE THREE BEARS (Easy)

Materials:
12-mesh canvas, 8-in. by 18-in.
Size 20 tapestry needle
1-1/2 oz. light brown Persian yarn,
    60 strands
1/2 oz. tan Persian yarn, 20 strands
3 strands white yarn
1 strand red yarn
9 black sequins
6 gold sequins
1/3 yd. velvet ribbon
Elastic cord
Brown felt, 8-in. by 18-in.

Directions:
Using patterns on pages 84-85, work bears in basketweave stitch. Work red trim on Mama Bear's cap from each edge to middle, leaving an end of yarn at center. Tie ends in a bow and cut desired length.

Finish according to general directions. Put a velvet bow on Baby Bear. Tie a velvet tie around Papa Bear's neck.

CANDY CANE (Easy)

Materials:
12-mesh canvas, 5-in. by 8-in.
Size 20 tapestry needle
12 strands white yarn
8 strands red yarn
3 strands dark red yarn
1 piece white felt, 5-in. by 8-in.
Elastic cord

Directions:
Using pattern on page 86, work in basketweave stitch. Finish according to general directions.

SANTA IN HIS HOUSE
(More Difficult)

Materials:
14-mesh canvas, 6-in. by 7-in.
Size 20 tapestry needle
9 strands white yarn
3 strands red yarn
1 strand dark red yarn
2 strands flesh yarn
1 strand gray yarn
1 strand blue yarn
1 strand pink yarn
1 strand light red yarn
8 strands green yarn
White felt, 6-in. by 7-in.

Directions:
Using pattern on page 86, work roof and ledge in upright gobelin stitch, tassle in turkey tufting or surrey stitch, all the rest in basketweave.

Omit stuffing. Back with white felt after finishing according to general directions.

FRENCH BOOT (More Difficult)

Materials:
12-mesh canvas, 5-in. by 6-in.
Size 20 tapestry needle
5 strands white yarn
6 strands pink yarn
6 strands red yarn
2 strands green yarn
1 strand red yarn
4 in. velvet ribbon or elastic cord
6 simulated pearls
Felt (white or desired color), 10-in.
    by 6-in.

Directions:
Using pattern on page 87, work design in basketweave. Make "buttonholes" by working three straight stitches over work. Sew on pearls. See general directions. Cut two pieces of felt for back. Sew one along top after attaching hanger. Lay on other piece and sew both to front with overcast stitch. This makes a lovely gift with a bottle of perfume inserted in stocking. Becomes ornament for the tree also.

ROCKING HORSE (More Difficult)

Materials:
12-mesh canvas, 6-in. by 6-in.
Size 20 tapestry needle
Felt, 6-in. by 6-in.
7 strands red yarn
8 strands green yarn
5 strands brown or black yarn

3 strands cream white yarn
2 ft. cloisonne metallic or pearl cotton
1 black sequin
8 colored sequins
4 in. elastic cord

Directions:
Using pattern on page 86, work in basketweave. Work mane and tail in surrey or turkey tufting. Omit pressing. Finish with felt backing and stuffing. Any color combination can be used.

ANGEL (Most Difficult)

Materials:
12-mesh canvas, 8-in. by 12-in.
Size 20 tapestry needle
1 oz. white yarn—40 strands
4 strands gold yarn
1 strand dark gold yarn
4 strands blue yarn
4 ft. silver metallic (cloisonne)
4 ft. gold metallic
3 strands flesh yarn
1 strand pink yarn
2 ft. florist's wire
1 sq. ft. iron-on suit interfacing

Directions:
Using pattern on page 88, follow general directions through pressing. Cut interfacing to fit finished back side. Lay short piece of wire on wings. Press interfacing on per directions. Sew up back of skirt by hand, turn, press seam open. Cover seam with more interfacing. Make halo by covering 6 in. of wire with gold metallic thread. Shape around small spool of thread and twist ends together. Fasten on back of head with more interfacing. Bend wings back.

Choosing the Tree

By Charlotte Carpenter
Sabetha, Kansas

THE TIMBER on our farm played an important part in my childhood in all seasons, but especially at Christmastime.

In the fall, when we gathered walnuts and hickory nuts from the timber for winter use, we collected acorns to make into tiny silver bells for Christ-

" . . . we argued and dreamed about which little evergreen would make the best Christmas tree . . ."

mas. Before the days grew cold, we also had to haul up wood from the piles we had sawed earlier.

During all of these trips to the timber we argued and dreamed about which little evergreen among the few that grew there would make the best Christmas tree. Our forest was full of deciduous trees, but these evergreens grew in a place we called the "bare spot".

The area was about a block square and afforded a good place for a rare picnic or weiner roast during the year.

The birds didn't seem to roost in this place or plant many of the evergreen seeds, but there was a cluster of five or six trees that did grow.

That Perfect Tree

Our childish eyes would spot a perfect tree and watch for it each time we passed by—dreaming of its beauty when it was trimmed with tinsel, baubles and real candles. We could envision it standing on our library table, next to the coal-oil lamp on top of the piano.

To this day I have never seen a more beautiful sight than the shadowy, dim glow of that lamp which lit up that tree as no electric light could.

Finally, when the great day drew near, our dad would take the axe and head for the timber, with great strides we could hardly match, to cut our

" . . . we pulled our sled along to carry the tree home . . ."

favorite tree. By that time we had all pretty well agreed on *the one*. If we were lucky, it had snowed and we pulled our sled along to carry the tree home.

Today, the choice of Christmas trees is almost endless. We may have

any size, or kind—if we want to pay the price. Artificial Christmas trees flood our market places . . . lifelike polyethylene, polyvinyl chloride, plastic, foil and styrene trees—in a price range of $5 to $100.

Available in every shade of green imaginable—moss, forest, deep or pine —they come equipped with folding branches and can be easily stored for use year after year. Mock Scotch Pine, Blue Spruce, Canadian Pine, Northern

" . . . the shadowy and dim reflection of that lamp lit that tree as no electric light can . . ."

Fir . . . the selection is endless. But, somehow there's nothing exciting about choosing from such an array.

I guess I miss that intangible, yet distinctive aroma that hit the nose at the first blow of the axe and lingered all the way home from the timber. Even after the tree had been taken down after Christmas, the scent of stray needles prolonged the pleasure.

More than anything, I think I miss the togetherness of a whole family choosing that special tree, and watching it grow through the seasons in our stand of timber so long ago.

J.E. SANFORD

Terrific Tree Trims

HANDMADE ornaments make your tree extra special. Above are four designs using pom-poms and felt. Colorful ornaments at left use felt glued on shapes cut from the foam trays many supermarkets use to package meat. Below, a calico fabric wreath gives the tree a country look.

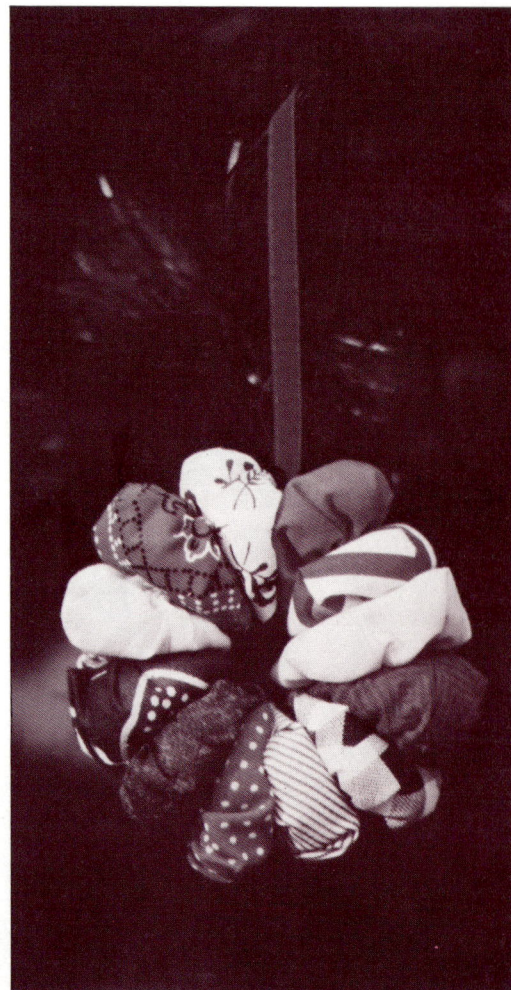

Perky Ornaments of Pom-Poms and Felt

By Mrs. Bernard Empen
Forreston, Illinois

LOOKING for some new, cheerful faces among your Christmas ornaments? Then you'll surely want to try making these four "personalities". They are easy to make and will delight youngsters as well as being good bazaar sellers.

SATIN POODLE BALL

Materials:
2-1/2-in. white satin ball with hook
Felt: white, red
White chenille pom-poms,
*   two 1-in., six 3/4-in.*
1/4 in. red chenille pom-pom
Small bow
Glue

Directions:
Cut two ears from white felt according to pattern and glue a 1-in. white chenille pom-pom about 1 in. from bottom of each ear. Glue ears to

---

These ornaments pictured on page 25, top right.

---

top of ball, one on each side. Glue four 3/4-in. white pom-poms in a circle around hook.

Glue on a tongue of red felt and a nose of two 3/4-in. white pom-poms side by side, with red one between them and just above the tongue. Top with a small bow on the hook.

TEDDY BEAR

Materials:
Felt, 2-1/2 by 3 in.
Two 1-in. chenille pom-poms
Four 3/4-in. chenille pom-poms
Three 1/2-in. chenille pom-poms
6 in. gold cord
Black felt scrap
Tiny moveable eyes
Small bow
Glue

Directions:
Cut teddy out of felt according to pattern on page 89. Loop cord for hanger and glue to top of felt, centered on head area. Glue on large pom-poms for head and body. Glue on medium pom-poms for legs and arms.

Glue on small pom-poms for ears and nose.

Glue on eyes and a tiny black felt circle for nose. Make a bow of narrow ribbon and glue in place at neck.

ESKIMO

Materials:
Felt: white, black, red, pink
10 in. gold cord
3 in. gold braid
8 in. fringe
Sequins: 6 red, 4 gold, 1 black
Tiny red bead
Glue
Stuffing

Directions:
Cut out felt pieces from pattern on page 89. Form hanger from 6 in. of the gold cord and glue to top of hood. Glue mittens and boots in place on front and back of hooded jacket. Stitch Eskimo front to Eskimo back, stuffing as you go.

Trim jacket with red felt strip glued down center front. Glue gold braid down center of strip and glue on 3 red sequin "buttons". Glue a piece of gold braid to end of each sleeve and trim with red sequins.

Glue a piece of fringe across jacket just below sleeves. Add a gold sequin to each boot.

Glue hair on head. Cut a black sequin in half for eyes and glue on. Glue on a half red sequin for mouth and tiny red bead for nose. Glue head into place and surround head with remaining fringe. Tie a bow from remaining gold cord and glue on just below chin.

Sew two sides of fish together, stuffing as you go. Then thread fish to mitten, leaving a little length of thread for fish to dangle. Glue gold sequin eye to each side of fish.

SANTA

Materials:
Felt: red, pink, white
6 in. gold cord
Moveable eyes
Stuffing
White chenille 1-in. pom-pom
Glue

Directions:
Cut out felt pieces from pattern on page 90. Form hanger with gold cord and glue to inside top of Santa's hat. Sew the two pieces of red felt together, leaving space at the bottom to stuff. Sew shut after stuffing.

Glue pink face into position, then white beard and hair. Glue on eyes and pom-pom.

Bird Carries Legend of Good Fortune

By Mary Jane Graybill
Stevens, Pennsylvania

I MADE over 50 of these Bird in a Nest ornaments last year and the children gave one to each of their school and Sunday School teachers. They enjoyed that more than a box of candy or perfume; so did my relatives and friends who received them.

Materials:
Excelsior paper
Paste
Gold spray paint
Clothespin
Florist's clay
Artificial flowers, fruit
Small bird

Directions:
Mix excelsior paper with paste and shape paper into nest. Allow to dry. Glue clothespin to bottom of nest. Spray nest and clothespin with gold paint. Let dry. Place a small piece of

(Continued on page 26)

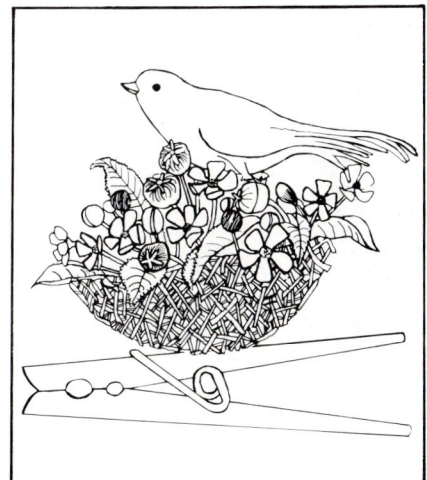

(Continued from page 25)
florist's clay in nest. Add flowers, greens, fruit, and finish with a pretty bird. You can attach a tag to the clothespin with this message:

A CHRISTMAS LEGEND

A bird in a nest of your Christmas tree is said to give you a year of happiness and good fortune.

Wreath Ornaments Made of Patchwork

By Carol Wahlen
Wauwatosa, Wisconsin

IF YOU'RE like most farm wives, you've collected a closetful of fabric remnants through your years of sewing. If you've been waiting for a craft project which is tailormade for your odds and ends, why not make patch-work wreaths this Christmas?

These wreaths are small enough to serve as tree ornaments or the perfect party favor, and all you have to do is enlarge the pattern to have a festive Christmas centerpiece.

Materials:
1-lb. plastic coffee can lid
Scrap fabric (red and green)
Cosmetic cotton balls
Tapestry needle
Fine cord or heavy string
Satin ribbon, 1/4 in. wide, 20 in. long

To make basic pattern, use plastic coffee can lid to trace a circle approximately 4 in. in diameter on fabric. Using this pattern, cut 12 fabric circles.

Turn under 1/4-in. hem around circle edges and baste down. Before cutting threads, fill fabric circle with cotton balls. Then, draw thread tightly, closing circle opening. Make knot and trim threads.

Thread tapestry needle with cord or string, knotting one end. Insert needle through center of individual balls, drawing together to form wreath.

Double ribbon length, and fold again, drawing needle with thread through midpoint of double ribbon length. Then, pull cord tightly and knot. Tie loose ends of ribbon into bow.

To make a larger wreath centerpiece, use a 2-lb. coffee can lid pattern.

Festive Figures Of Felt and Foam

By Eleanor Nolin
Cissna Park, Illinois

THESE decorations, made from foam trays, are fun to make and can be used on your tree, on packages or even sent as Christmas cards with "Merry Christmas" and your name written on the back with a felt tip pen.

I save the foam trays that I get with meat, fruit, etc. in the grocery store. I wash them and cut off the edge with a scissors. Now I am ready for the patterns. Several are shown on pages 93-97. I traced some of the others, like the pig and rabbit, from coloring books. Why not try these, then have fun coming up with your own designs?

Materials:
Foam trays
Single-edged razor blade
Glue
String or cord
Tapestry or yarn needle
Felt in color indicated on patterns
*   or Christmas cards*

Directions:
Trace the outline for the various ornaments on the foam tray and cut out with the razor blade. Cut felt as indicated and glue on to ornament. Thread needle with decorative string or cord and push needle through ornament near top. Tie ends to form hanger.

To make ornaments with Christmas card designs, tear picture from a Christmas card and glue onto piece of foam tray. Using the razor blade, cut around design, leaving about 1/8 in. of tray showing. Thread hanger through.

Clothespin Dolls Dress Up the Tree

By Louella Sanders
Houston, Texas

PICK some of your prettiest fabric, trim and ribbon scraps to make clothespin dolls to hang on your Christmas tree. Your older children will also enjoy this project.

Materials:
Round-topped clothespin
Scraps: fabric, trim, ribbon,
*   felt, lightweight yarn*
Paints
Gesso or thick flour/water mix
Glue

Directions:

Dip knob end of clothespin, including neck, in three coats gesso; let dry. Paint on face. Tightly braid three strands yarn about 7 in. long. Tie ends of braid with ribbon bows. Glue on hair in middle of head. Glue on small round disc of felt for hat.

Take a strip of fabric 6 in. wide and 12 in. long and fold to 6-in. square (fold will be skirt bottom). Sew along each side to 1-1/2 in. of fold. Turn. Tack in rough edges at opening near fold (this opening may be used for holding coins, candy, small gifts, etc.). Hem a small casing at top and run a narrow ribbon through it.

Trim bottom of skirt as desired. Insert doll pin and draw tightly, leaving head and neck showing. Knot this ribbon and use long end to hang doll on tree. Draw in waist and tie with ribbon.

PRETTY CLOTHESPIN DOLLS can be made with fabric and trim scraps from your sewing box. Make them simple or fancy—they'll be an interesting addition to your tree. And, you might want to keep this idea in mind for your next bazaar project.

Personalized Ornaments: Great Project for Kids

By Rosalyn Goodman
Northbrook, Illinois

EVEN A CHILD can enjoy making personalized Christmas tree ornaments easily and inexpensively. All you need to furnish is construction paper, pencil, scissors, glue, a stack of old newspapers and magazines, needle and thread.

Egg-citing Idea For Your Tree

By Mrs. Ryno Olson
Muscatine, Iowa

BLOWN-OUT eggs with handpainted designs make delightful ornaments for your Christmas tree. These eggs would also be great as gifts for your friends and relatives who look for many different "collectible" ornaments for their trees.

Materials:
Egg
Corsage pin
Clear acrylic spray
Graphite paper
Paint (oil or acrylics)

8 in. gold or silver cord
Velvet ribbon or other trim

Directions:
Blow out egg so largest hole is at top end. To make blowing easier, break yolk with corsage pin. Spray clear acrylic on egg and allow to dry. Transfer the design of your choice to egg with graphite paper. (Do not use pencil for design—lead will get into your paint.) I use two designs on each egg. Paint with oil or acrylic paints. Oil-painted eggs require a week or more to dry. Knot cording and push knot into top hole on egg. Glue velvet ribbon or other trim around egg.

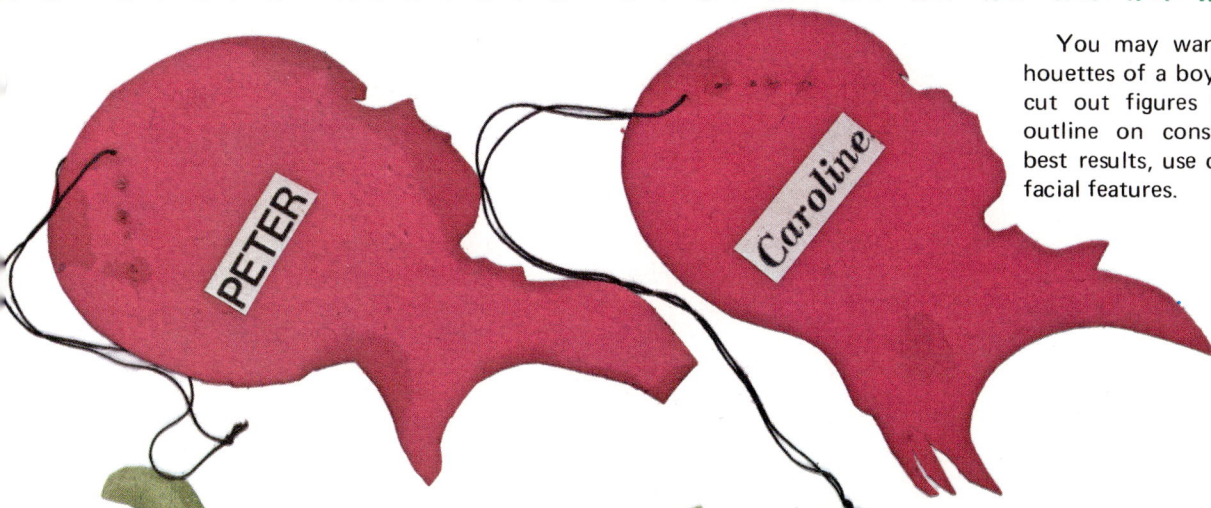

You may want to trace these silhouettes of a boy and girl. To do this, cut out figures from this page, and outline on construction paper. For best results, use cuticle scissors to cut facial features.

PETER

Caroline

HARRIS

Surprise your friends and relatives by placing their names on this Christmas candle.

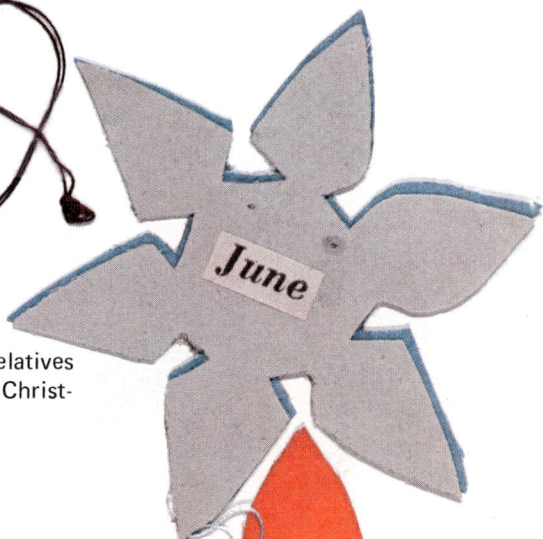

June

These silhouettes can be used for adult members of the family.

FATHER

Karen

Directions:

Hunt through magazines and newspapers (or the phone book) for names of family members. Cut out names and make a family circle ornament. Dot the back of names with glue, and paste them on colored construction paper. Using a drinking glass, trace a circle around names. Cut out circle. Thread a needle and push needle through top of circle.

Pull out 3 or 4 in., snip, and knot the ends of thread. You can also punch a hole with a pin and use a string to hang ornament on tree branch.

A cookie cutter was used to shape this ornament of the family dog.

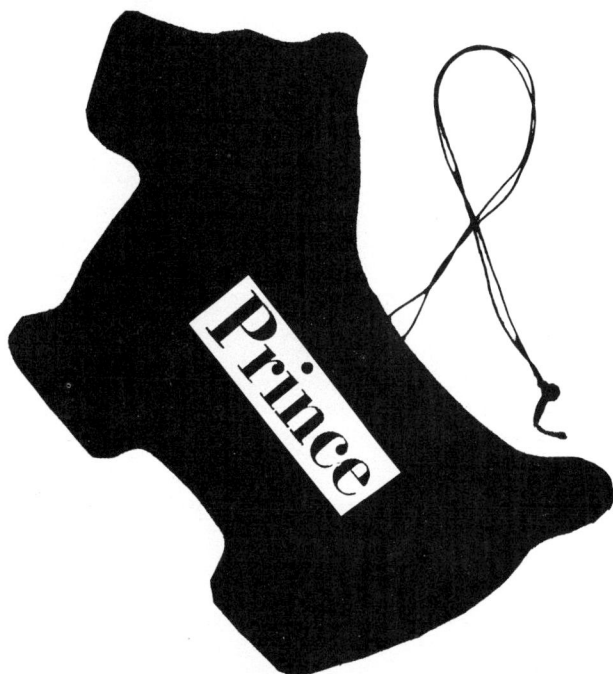

For a family mobile, trace and cut out two snowflakes for each name in the same or contrasting color. Scraps of Christmas wrap also can be used for the backing.

Cut out and paste names in center of snowflakes. Line up nameless snowflakes in a row. Dab glue on top and bottom points and in the center.

Measure and cut a piece of thread slightly longer than twice the length of the row. Double thread, leaving a loop at top.

Hold the loop above the first snowflake, and lay thread down the row so it touches glue.

Dot backs of the "named" snowflakes with glue, and press each one over string. Allow to dry.

The ABCs of Christmas

A *is for the agony of Christmas shopping,*
 The pushing, the rushing, the packages dropping.
B *is for bruises from scrubbing the floors,*
 Dusting the walls and polishing the doors.
C *is for cookies so carefully made,*
 Now all devoured by a massive raid.
D *is for decorations tattered and worn.*
 The wreath is now shabby and the bell is quite torn.
E *is for energy, and it takes quite a bit,*
 To keep the refrig' well stocked and the homes fires lit.
F *is for the food which converts into fat,*
 Pot lucks will do it in one week flat.
G *is for games piled high in the store,*
 Finding "Authors" or "Uncle Wiggly" is now a real chore.
H *is for houseguests soon to arrive.*
 Hoping by Christmas we'll still be alive.
I *is for ironing doubled in size,*
 Blouses and slacks and polka dot ties.
J *is for the joy of wrapping odd-shaped presents,*
 An ironing board, folding chairs, and two frozen pheasants.
K *is for kids, overly excited,*
 So many commercials make their decisions misguided.
L *is the list of items I must remember to bring,*
 To dinners and parties and every such thing.
M *is for money which vanishes in air,*
 A few dollars here and a few dollars there.
N *is for newspapers with pages of ads,*
 Urging me to buy all the latest in fads.
O *is for ornaments so fragile and thin,*
 More delicate to touch than baby's skin.
P *is for programs which must be attended,*
 'else children and teachers be deeply offended.
Q *is for quality often hard to find,*
 An open seam here, a toy that won't wind.
R *is for that ransacked look on Christmas morn,*
 When gifts are opened and paper is torn.
S *is for spasms which persist in my fingers,*
 The pain of writing cards and notes still lingers.
T *is for the lopsided tree,*
 Which has tipped over twice on me.
U *is for under-the-bed where gifts are stashed,*
 Desperately hoping nothing gets smashed.
V *is for vacation the kiddies have from school,*
 A long time for mothers to keep their cool!
W *is for the weather, bitter and cold,*
 More mittens and snow boots than the kitchen can hold.
X *is for Xmas, that one day in December,*
 When children play, fathers relax, and mothers remember.
Y *is for yoo-hoo when Christmas is over,*
 When the house is in order and all is in clover.
Z *is for the zest which must be replaced,*
 Before a new year and another Christmas can be faced!

By Vera Heithoff
Elgin, Nebraska

Christmas Fun for the Kids

By Mildred Grenier, St. Joseph, Missouri

From Our Farm To Yours...

Outlined by window frame I see
    Soft snow flakes flock a green fir tree;
Three red bird candles flicker bright
    In blue and gold of falling night;
Inside the barn, such as He lay,
The cattle low and munch sweet hay.
    Above the pine by pasture bar
Evening leans down and lights a star . . .
    Footprints the birds and rabbits drew
Spell out our season's wish for you;
    With snow piled high on lot and yard,
God paints our country Christmas card.

—Mildred Grenier

Stitch Up a Poinsettia Pot Scrubber

A POINSETTIA Pot Scrubber is certain to give your kitchen sink a holiday lift. You make these poinsettias any size you wish, but I make mine by cutting three pieces of dark green net into 4-in. squares.

Stacking these so the points do not overlap, stitch firmly with needle and thread through the center. Cut three bright red nylon net squares 4 in. in

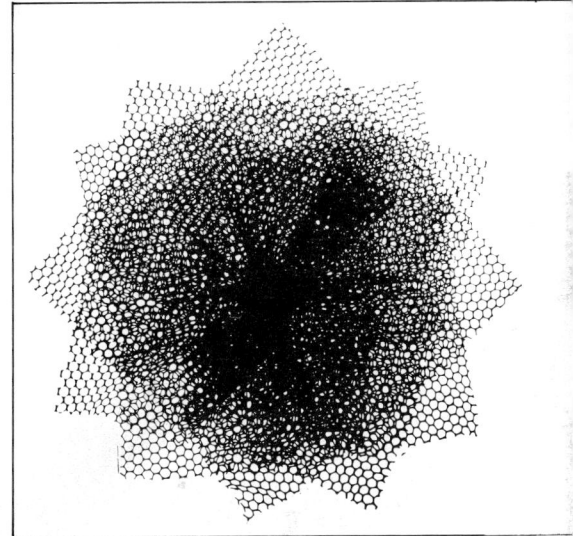

size, again stacking these so that the points don't overlap.

Then, stitch a circle in the center and pull up like a drawstring so the red net resembles a flower. Fasten this firmly with needle and thread to the green nylon net "leaves". For the finishing touches, make several large French knots with embroidery thread in the center of the red flower.

Make a Frosty Centerpiece

CHILDREN LOVE to make these glittering winter centerpieces. First, fill a glass jar, clear glass bowl or water glass one-half full of salt. Stick evergreen tips into the salt, and set the glass, jar or bowl in a shallow dish or plate.

Fill the glass or jar to overflowing with water, adding water as the water evaporates. Salt crystals will form on the dish and tree, resembling sparkling frost or snow.

You'll find you can make strikingly beautiful centerpieces by adding small reindeer, sleighs, churches, carolers and other small figurines.

You Can't "Pan" This Skillet Centerpiece

TIE A RED ribbon on a pretty, shiny aluminum or copper skillet. Fill skillet with greens and place a large red or green candle in the midst of the skillet greenery.

Add pine cones, Christmas balls or bright red berries for accent. Now, be prepared for the cheery smiles that will greet your uniquely beautiful kitchen centerpiece.

You Can't "Beat" These Christmas Drums!

THESE DRUMS may be filled with cookies, candy or other goodies to make a "striking" Christmas present. Children love to play with these drums after they're emptied as well!

Cover a 1-lb. coffee can with red felt, cut-to-fit and glued on. Glue heavy white cord to the can, making the familiar criss-cross effect around the sides of the drum.

Then, glue a 1-in.-wide strip of black felt or ribbon around the top and bottom of the drum. To complete the effect, attach two real drumsticks, or two sticks of candy as drumsticks with each drum that you give.

Quick-Knit Tree Makes Merry Holiday Hanging

By Mary Lamb Becker
Milwaukee, Wisconsin

THIS CHRISTMAS tree is a quick-to-knit project made from a new yarn called Maxi-Cord, a super-bulky, 8-ply, 100% synthetic yarn available through your craft or hobby shop. The gauge for this pattern is 4 stitches = 3 inches; 2 rows = 1 inch. The tree can be knit in about 3 or 4 hours if you are an average knitter. The finishing will take just a little longer.

Materials:

90 yd. bright green Maxi-Cord
8-1/2 yd. white Maxi-Cord
1-1/2 yd. red Maxi-Cord
3/4 yd. 72-in. green felt
12 red wooden beads, 7/8-in. diameter
2 pieces scrap cardboard,
*   22 in. x 25 in., 6 in. x 22 in.*
1 pair 14-in. size 17 knitting needles or whatever size you need to come to gauge. (Note: If you want to make your own needles, 1/2-in. wooden doweling is the equivalent of size 17 needles. Taper the ends with a knife and sand smooth. No other finish is necessary.)

Directions: Cast on 3 stitches. Row 1: knit. Row 2: purl. Row 3: k1, pick up horizontal yarn to right of center stitch, twist it clockwise and slip on left needle. Knit horizontal yarn as a stitch. Knit center stitch. Pick up horizontal yarn to left of center stitch, twist clockwise and slip on left needle. Knit horizontal yarn as a stitch. Knit

last stitch. (5 sts.)

Row 4: purl. Row 5: knit. Row 6: purl. Row 7: k2, increase 1 st on either side of center st as in Row 3, k2 (7 sts).

Continue shaping tree by increasing every fourth row, making one increase on either side of the center stitch. After 11 increase rows you will have 25 stitches. This is Row 43. Purl next row, knit next two rows. Bind off.

To knit tree base, cast on 2 sts. Row 1: knit. Row 2: purl. Row 3: k1, inc once in last st (3 sts). Row 4: purl. Row 5: k2, inc one in last st (4 sts).

Repeat increase every fourth row three times more (7 sts). This last increase row is Row 17. Row 18: purl. Row 19: knit. (Row 19 is center of base piece.) Row 20: purl. Row 21: k5, k2 tog (6 sts).

Continue to decrease one stitch every fourth row three times more. This last decrease row is Row 33 (3 sts). Row 34: purl. Row 35: k1, k2 tog (2 sts). Row 36: purl. Bind off allowing about 2 yd. of yarn for sewing. Cut yarn.

To assemble, lay two knit pieces flat on green felt. Draw around both shapes with chalk. Cut out felt allowing 1-in. seam allowances. Press under seam allowances. Cut out one piece of cardboard same shape as knitted base piece.

Sew curved edge of knit base piece to lower edge of knit tree, easing where necessary. Glue or staple cardboard base piece to felt base, bringing

seam allowances to wrong side. Sew curved edge of felt base piece to felt tree just as with knit pieces.

Next, lay joined felt pieces over enough fiber fill (or other stuffing) to fill out shape. Place felt and filling on cardboard and trace around shape with pencil. This will be a triangular-shaped piece slightly narrower than when the piece lay flat.

Cut out cardboard along pencil lines. Cut identical piece of felt but allow 1-in. seam allowances on all sides. Cover tree-shaped cardboard piece with felt as you did with the base piece, glueing or stapling in place.

Sew the joined felt pieces to covered cardboard by hand, allowing opening for stuffing. Stuff and sew opening closed. Place knitted pieces over felt tree and sew in place along outer edge using sewing thread.

To make garland, use white Maxi-Cord and knot to simulate popcorn. Drape swags of garland on tree. Attach with white sewing thread.

Ornaments: Cut 1-1/2 yd. red Maxi-Cord into 18-in. lengths. Separate into 4-ply strands. This will give you six 4-ply strands each 18 in. long. Thread one 4-ply strand through large-eye needle. String two beads, catch one or two loops of the tree, return through beads in reverse order. Pull yarn ends even, slide beads up to tree, knot just below beads. Trim yarn ends.

Tree will stand upright. If you prefer, you can make a loop at top of tree for hanging.

Festive Burlap Hanging Heralds the Holidays

By Carol Missling
Owen, Wisconsin

ADD a strip of Christmas color to your wall or door with this bright burlap hanging, decorated with felt and cotton fringe balls.

The fringe balls are from trim you can buy by the yard at the fabric store. I used the large balls (1-in. diameter) and medium balls 3/4-in. diameter). You can use the designs I did or create some of your own.

Materials:
White burlap, 10-1/2 by 46 in.
Felt squares:
    dark green, 2
    light green
    pink
    purple
    red
Fringe balls:
    olive green, 10 med., 4 large
    red, 7 med., 7 large
    pink, 10 med.
    orange, 6 med.
    red/white/green, 7 large
48 in. heavy white yarn
Gold glitter
Glue
Dowel, 9-1/2 in. long

Directions:
Cut piece of burlap straight on all sides. Fringe the two long sides and bottom 1 in. by pulling threads. To prevent piece from fraying more, stitch along fringe sides on machine.

Hem 1 in. at top to form casing.

Divide burlap into six sections by gluing on 1/2-in. by 7-in. strips of dark green felt. Cut felt designs according to patterns on page 99. Glue on patterns and ball fringe as indicated. Glue gold glitter on candle flame.

Cut heavy yarn into three 16-in. strands. Insert dowel into casing. Braid yarn and tie onto ends of dowel to form handle.

Floor Your Friends With A Mop Santa

By Mrs. Robert Lindberg
Sebeka, Minnesota

THIS Christmas, why not make your own Mop Santa to hang on your wall or door? This simple decoration is made from a dust mop, Christmas tree ornament balls, pom-pom and red cotton cloth.

Materials:
2 blue Christmas tree balls
    (1-1/2-in. diameter)
1 red Christmas ball (2-in. diameter)
1 white yarn dust mop
1 small white pom-pom
1/2 yd. red cotton material
Red thread

Directions:
Make red Santa cap out of cotton material, according to pattern on page 00. Sew 1/4-in. seam along curved edge and hem 1/2 in. at bottom edge. Fit cap over top of mop and fasten along backside.

Fold tip of cap down diagonally and tack at lower edge of the fold. Attach small white pom-pom to tip of hat. Fasten blue and red Christmas balls in place on mop to form face. Make loop on backside of cap to hang.

Use pearls and beads to make . . .

Jewel of a Christmas Tree

By Cheryl Taylor
Heyworth, Illinois

THIS PEARL DROP Christmas tree plaque will add a delicate touch to your holiday decor. All you need is a gilded picture frame or mirror, fabric, pearls and beads.

Materials:
Frame (bubbled glass or recessed back at least 1/4 in. deep so beads fit)
Brocade fabric
Dark green velvet
3mm strung pearl beads
Pearl drops
Gold-plated oval beads
Tree pattern (from Christmas card or make your own)
Glue that dries clear
Tweezers
Small piece of wood for trunk

Directions:
Cut cardboard to fit frame. Glue brocade to cardboard and place under a heavy object so it will be flat. When dry (20 to 30 min.), cut excess brocade from cardboard.

Cut out velvet tree and glue on brocade. Place it slightly above the center of cardboard so it will be centered when you add the trunk.

Drape strung beads by placing thin line of glue on velvet, then place beads, using tweezers, to form corners. Place additional single pearls, pearl drops and gold oval beads as you wish.

To make star on top, glue on a single 3mm pearl and 5 gold oval beads around it to resemble a flower.

Poinsettias of Burlap Burst Into Bloom

By Mrs. Jim Torrance
Good Hope, Illinois

HERE'S another idea for making your own poinsettia plant this Christmas season. All you need is burlap, chenille strips, wire, glue and tape—and a little holiday spirit!

Materials:
Red burlap (5-1/2 by 36 in. makes 18 petals)
Green burlap (2-1/2 by 1-1/2-in.) (or artificial flower center)
Red chenille strips
Stem wire
Glue
Florist tape

Directions:
Trace petal pattern on red burlap. Glue chenille stem on pattern and let dry. Cut out petals.

To make center, pull strings out of 1-1/2-in. side of green burlap, leaving 1/2-in. solid. Roll piece up lightly.

Bend top of wire stem to make crook, and push this through burlap flower center near bottom. Fit five petals around center and wrap tightly with florist tape.

Now open petals and shape, slightly pinching outside ends to achieve the poinsettia look. Arrange in bouquet, using artificial greenery.

Rejuvenate old jewelry for Christmas by using the pearls and beads to make a framed wallhanging.

Christmas Wreaths With Country Charm

Straw Wreath

Burlap Wreath

Tuna Can Wreath

Country Wreath

Burlap Wreath

By Mrs. Ernest Bartels
Peshtigo, Wisconsin

FOR A doorway wreath which will withstand the wintry Yuletide season, try making this surprisingly realistic burlap Christmas wreath. All you need is a wire coat hanger and a few yards of green burlap.

Materials:
1 wire coat hanger
1-1/3 yard 54-in. burlap or
2 yards 36-in. burlap

Directions:
Cut burlap into eight 6-in. strips, across the width of material. (Cut 12 strips for 36-in. material.) Fringe 18 rows on each side of strip. (First cut off selvage on both ends.) Undo coat hanger and form into circle.

Thread burlap strips at 1/2-in. intervals on hanger. When strips have been threaded on hanger, twist to give further fullness. Braid 18 strands of raveled thread and use this braid to cover hanger hook. Trim as desired—with small Christmas ornaments, holly, or ribbon.

Straw Wreath

By Roylinda Rumbaugh
Mattawan, Michigan

UPON opening my craft shop, "The Lean-To", I had many requests for straw wreaths. These wreaths can be decorated for Christmas or any season of the year.

My favorite way to decorate is to wrap gingham ribbon around the wreath, not covering it completely. In the spaces where the straw shows through, add clusters of strawflowers or other decorations and as a finishing touch, a big, fluffy gingham bow. This is how I make the wreaths:

Materials:
Rounded foam wreath (any diameter)
Firm, fresh straw
Fishing line
Cornhusks
Pins

Directions:
Wrap cornhusks around wreath form to cover, using pins to hold husks in place. This covers the wreath so no white or green shows through.

Take one nice handful of long straw and wrap lengthwise around the wreath. Tie with line at one end of straw and continue wrapping with line until you reach the end of that section of straw. Add another handful of straw and wrap with line again. Continue wrapping straw until you reach your starting point. Tie securely and add a loop of line for a hanger.

You may then tie every so often with cornhusk if you want a more primitive-looking wreath. Wreath is now ready to decorate as you choose.

Tuna Can Wreath

By Georgia Goldsberry
St. Joseph, Missouri

YOU CAN make a wreath for your front door easily and quickly using tuna or catfood cans. It offers a bright welcome, and at practically no cost!

Materials:
9 catfood or tuna cans
Tape
Spray paint, green or gold
9 pine cones
Paint for cones
Glitter
Epoxy glue
Bright bow
Cord for hanger

Directions:
Remove tops and bottoms of cans and soak cans to remove labels. Now tape cans together to form a wreath. Spray paint the wreath. Next spray or brush paint nine pine cones in whatever color you choose. Sprinkle on some glitter while the paint is still wet. When the pine cones are dry, use epoxy glue to glue one in the bottom of each of the rings formed by the cans. Tie on a bright bow, add a hanger and your wreath is ready to hang.

Country Wreath

By Joyce Matich
Chicago, Illinois

WHY NOT let your Christmas decor go "haywire" this year? Simply decorate your door with this colorful country wreath, made from hay, ribbon, cornhusks and wire. "Doll up" your wreath with your own homemade cornhusk doll.

Materials:
Hay or straw
Strong string
3 yards of ribbon
Cornhusks and cornhusk doll
Stapler
Wire and florist picks

Directions:
Gather hay and wrap tightly with string to form a wreath. Cut a wide ribbon into 5- to 6-in. pieces. Do the same with the cornhusks and bend each in half. Do not crease. Staple ends together.

Using florist picks, attach one cornhusk and one ribbon together. Continue this procedure around the wreath. Attach a big bow at the bottom with wire. Make or purchase a cornhusk doll and wire it to the center of the wreath.

Della Robbia Wreaths You Can Make Yourself

By Sharen Neumann Kaatz
Frederick, Wisconsin

If you always admired the Della Robbia wreaths in stores and catalogs, but never thought that you could afford to own one—now you can! Here's how you can make your own "poor man's" Della Robbia wreath.

Materials:
Styrofoam wreath form
Plastic fruits (medium-sized)
Nut shells
Assorted-size pine cones
6 to 8 bunches boxwood branches
Wire
Glue (make sure glue will not melt Styrofoam)
Wood picks

Directions:

Spray your wreath green, using a paint made especially for plastic. Begin with the boxwood, pushing it into the foam wreath in equal portions on all sides. Next, fill the inside of the hole and the front of the wreath with boxwood.

Add the fruit, alternating colors and kinds, filling the front of your wreath. If you are using walnut shells, first empty them and reglue with wood picks for mounting. Drill a hole and glue in a wood pick for pecans.

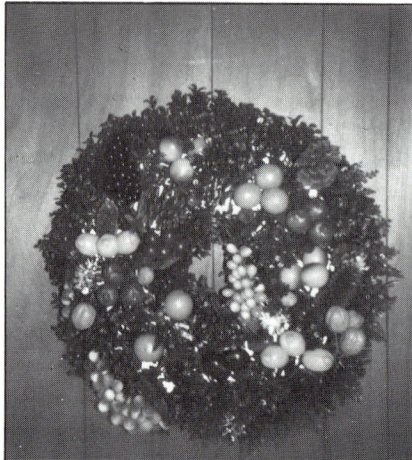

To prepare pine cones, paint with gold or aluminum paint and wind stiff wire around the stem end for mounting. Add the nuts and pine cones to give your Della Robbia wreath the finishing touches.

Hang the wreath with a strip of green cloth tied into a loop and attached to the top of the wreath. Store your Della Robbia wreath in a large plastic bag to protect it from dust.

Epsom Salt for Frosted Effect

By Maria Southworth
Lynnwood, Washington

ANOTHER VERSION of the popular Della Robbia wreath features sparkling plastic flowers, unusual textured peach stones and walnut shells and a layer of Epsom salt which gives the wreath a frosted effect.

Materials:
9-in. Styrofoam wreath
12 wired peach stones
18 empty, wired walnut shells
24 colored plastic flowers and leaves
Small plastic fruits (optional)
Glue that dries clear
1 cup Epsom salt
No. 18 wire

Drill, ice pick or steel knitting needle
1 yd. red ribbon
Fabric hanger
Stiff brush

Directions:

Glue fabric hanger to back of wreath.

Before wiring peach stones, lay stones in undiluted household bleach for about 5 minutes. When bleach begins to foam, take stones out and brush off all small particles with stiff brush. Rinse stones in warm water.

To attach piece of wire, drill hole about 1/2 in. deep through bottom of each peach stone. If no drill is available, use hot ice pick or steel needle to make small holes immediately after stones have been soaked. Use glue to fasten wires in stones.

To prepare walnut shells, pry the nuts apart with a sharp knife and empty the nuts. Glue the shell together and insert a short piece of wire before gluing together.

Cut stem of each flower to approximately 2 in. Thin glue with sparing amount of water. Brush glue on flowers and leaves, then sprinkle generous amount of Epsom salt over them. Do not shake off excess salt until glue has completely dried.

To decorate wreath, dip flower stems and peach stone wires into glue and insert them into the wreath as follows:

(a) one row around outside of wreath

(b) one row around inside of wreath, completely covering available area

(c) Divide space left empty in middle of wreath into four sections for good balance of design. Starting at top section, and working in only one direction, insert decorations in Styrofoam ring. Larger decorations should be placed at the four dividing points.

When finished, make large ribbon bow and fasten to wreath.

MORE PINE CONES are used in this version of a Della Robbia wreath, made by Mrs. R. M. Gustafson of Marquette, Neb. She drilled holes in the cones to insert 2-in. pipe cleaners with Tacky Glue then inserted other end of pipe cleaner into Styrofoam wreath form. She lined inner and outer edge of wreath with cones. Smaller cones, fruit and nuts complete the wreath.

Decorative Plaques Make Great Gifts

By Mrs. Freda Grones
Santa Ana, California

FOR EVERY Mr. and Mrs. on my family Christmas list, I am making a set of personalized decorative wood plaques to grace the walls of their home. The plaques are easy to make, and I've found that I can complete several sets in two evenings of work.

Materials:
2 matching wood shapes
Plastic or fabric flowers with
    flexible stems or clusters of
    short-stemmed red berries
Paint or stain
Staple gun
Rubber cement
Floral wire
Metal screw-in hanger
Red felt tip pen

Directions:

Spray, stain or brush color of your choice on plaque and allow to dry overnight. Attach flowers, using staple gun to secure long-stemmed flowers to the wood. Place staple across stem near head or under leaf, where it won't show. You also may want to dab rubber cement on underside of flower, leaves and stem.

When using buds or berries, divide them into two equal bunches and tie each bunch tightly in the middle with a bit of floral wire. Arrange the bunches on plaque and use two or three staples to hold each bunch in place. Bend buds forward—toward the center.

Attach metal screw-on hanger to back of each plaque, and use red felt-tip pen to inscribe a personal Christmas greeting on the back of one of the plaques of the set.

TO MAKE these plaque sets, simply choose your wood shapes, finish the wood with paint or stain and attach flowers or berries with a staple gun, as in photo at right. Bend berries to center and staple is hidden. When using long-stemmed flowers, as in photo above, place staple near head of flower or under a leaf to hide it. They make great gifts.

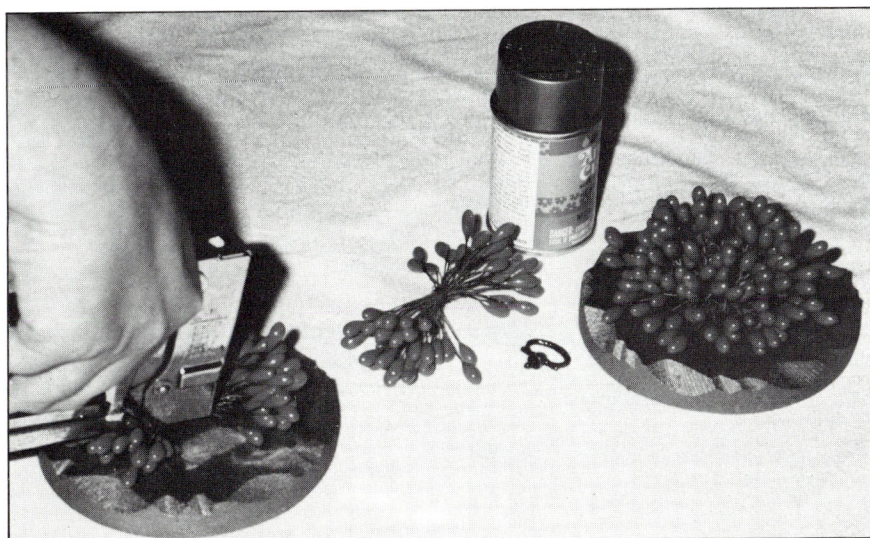

Recycle Lye Bottles Into Cluster of Bells

By Lois Costomiris
Cicero, Indiana

RING OUT the Christmas spirit with a cluster of these Christmas bells, constructed from white plastic lye containers.

Materials:

White plastic lye container
White glue
Decorative tapes, such as
*   rick-rack or metallic cord*
Ice pick or nail

24 to 36 in. rug yarn
Small Christmas balls

Directions:

Remove paper identification from containers. Wash containers thoroughly in hot water containing 1/2 cup vinegar to neutralize any lye inside. Let dry.

Cut bottom of cans away. Ring cans with a line of white glue to secure decorations. Stretch decorative tapes to form patterns on bell. Pin till dry.

Snap lid on. (The red-lid brand adds color.)

Push a hole through lid with ice pick or nail.

Double 24-in. to 36-in. length of rug yarn and string on small Christmas ball for clapper. Tie knot next to clapper-ball.

Thread yarn through lid hole and adjust so the clapper is slightly visible.

Form several bells into cluster, then knot yarn strings.

Fasten to branch of evergreen and hang on door or above fireplace.

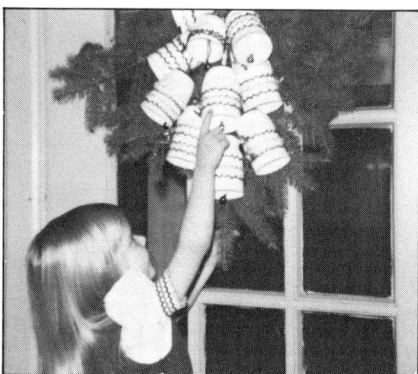

Tuna Tree's No Fish Story

By Mrs. Robert Lindberg
Sebeka, Minnesota

IF TUNA FISH is your family's favorite dish, why not save your empty cans to make a tuna can tree this Christmas? Your friends will "fish" for excuses to visit your home to see your unique tree.

Materials:

15 tuna cans (6-1/2-oz.)
15 small Christmas ball ornaments
Small piece of dowel

(1-1/4-in. diameter)
Gold or silver spray paint
Liquid solder
Wood glue
Board for base (3/4 in. thick,
*   8 in. long, 1-3/4 in. wide)*
Board for stand (19 in.)

Directions:

Drill shallow hole in base board for dowel. Insert dowel and glue into hole. Glue other end of dowel to middle of 19-in. board for stand. Approximately 2-3/4 in. of dowel should extend between stand and base for cans.

Solder all 15 cans into place, beginning with 5 cans on the bottom row and stacking each row with one less each time, in pyramid style. Remove wires from Christmas ornament balls and solder to top midpoint of each tuna can. Make sure that wires are positioned so that ornaments will hang straight within can.

Spray paint entire tree with gold or silver, and when it dries, attach the Christmas ornaments to soldered wires.

Ruffle Trees From Your Fabric Scraps

By Jean Leaman
Cochranville, Pennsylvania

NOW YOU can have your own Christmas tree farm! All you need is some red or green fabric from your scrap bag, a Styrofoam cone and a pair of pinking shears to create your own forest of ruffled Christmas trees.

Materials:

Styrofoam cone
Fabric
Pinking shears
Needle and thread
Straight pins
Tree top decorations

Directions:

Using the pinking shears, cut fabric into 1½-in. strips, piecing to obtain sufficient length if necessary. Take threaded needle and gather strips on the top edges.

Fit ruffle around bottom of cone, leaving a little lap, and adjusting gathers to the fullness you desire. Use a straight pin to fasten lapped edges to tree, and place one or two more pins along top edge of ruffle to hold it in place.

Position the next ruffle so that it covers the gathering thread of the previous ruffle. Keep all overlapped edges at the same point on your tree, forming the back of your tree. Top finished tree with matching or contrasting small tree ornaments.

By Mrs. Omar S. Stoutner
Keota, Iowa

KIDS LOVE to receive this red felt Santa Boot filled with cookies or candy at Christmas. I mail one each year to my grandkids who call it "Grandma's Santa Boot".

Materials:
Coffee can or oatmeal box
Red felt
White felt
Cord or yarn
Cotton or paper towels

Directions:
Trace pattern pieces on pages 105-108 and cut. Attach white cuff to red rectangle to form body of boot, keeping slanted corners at top edge. Sew toe-tongue section to fronts of boot at points A and B.

Pin sole to bottom of this round piece, placing toe at front of sole oval. Make adjustments by trimming sole to fit. Sew together with whip stitch by hand or zig-zag on machine.

Punch hole at dot marked on cuff and insert can. Tie together with cord or yarn and stuff toe with cotton or paper towels to obtain shape of a foot. Glue a circle of felt to top of coffee can.

Give a Bootful of Goodies

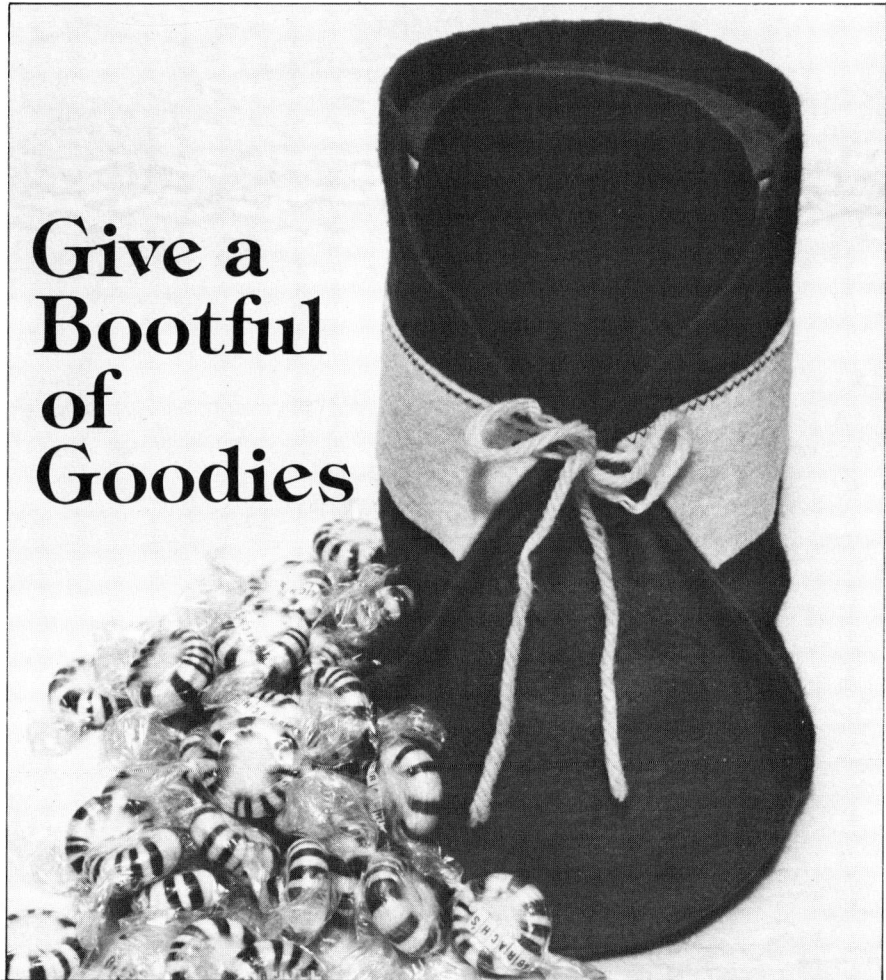

Basket Holds Cards, Gifts

By Ann Kaiser
Brookfield, Wisconsin

A BASKETFUL of holiday wishes can be a bright spot in your home this Christmas season. When Christmas cards arrive from friends and relatives, keep them together in this special card basket. It's attractive as well as convenient.

Why not make several and give them as gifts, filled with fruit, baked goods or other small items?

Materials:
Basket 9 in. in diameter
(1/2-peck size)
Gold spray paint
24 in. heavy wire
30 in. red velvet ribbon,
1-1/2 in. wide
27 in. red velvet ribbon,
1 in. wide
36 in. wired red velvet ribbon,
1-1/4 in. wide
Gold cord
27 in. narrow gold braid
60 in. wide gold braid
3 sprigs artificial holly
Green coated wire

Directions:
Spray basket inside and out with gold paint. Insert ends of heavy wire between inner top band and basket at opposite sides, to form handle. Turn up ends around bottom of band to secure.

Put some glue on end of gold cord and tightly wrap handle with cord, gluing other end to secure when handle is covered.

Glue 1-1/2-in. ribbon around top band and 1-in. ribbon around center band of basket. Glue narrow gold braid around at midpoint of narrow velvet ribbon. Glue wide gold braid on wide ribbon around top band, and around top of basket rim.

With wired ribbon, form two bows. Wire bows and holly sprigs (two sprigs on one side, one on the other) to handle at each side with green wire or decorate as you choose.

Hang Colorful Card Balls

By Julia Cunniff
Alstead, New Hampshire

CHRISTMAS card balls make pretty decorations for the tree or can add color and cheer hanging on a door or in a window. So get out last year's cards and get the whole family involved in making these easy decorations.

Materials:
Old Christmas cards
Stapler
Paper punch
Ribbon or yarn

Directions:

Cut 20 circles about 2-1/2 in. diameter out of the Christmas cards, using the focal point of card design in the circle. Fold each circle in at least three places so the center of each circle is shaped like a triangle (see diagram). 10 circles with point of triangle at top of design, 10 with point at bottom.

Staple five circles together so the points of the triangles meet together at the top. Then staple 10 circles together and to the top five circles, alternating point, at base and at top, making sure all pictures are right side up.

Staple the last five circles together (points at bottom) and to the 10 circles to complete the ball.

Punch holes in two of the top circles and thread through yarn or ribbon for hanger.

Holiday Placemats of Old Christmas Cards

By Dorothy Jones
Towanda, Illinois

ATTRACTIVE Christmas placemats can be made inexpensively by using "pre-sent" Christmas cards or Christmas wrapping paper. Your children will have fun with this project, too.

The mats will bring to mind the joys and blessings of the season at each meal. These mats are very durable and, with care, can be used several seasons.

Materials:
Cardboard, 11 by 16 in.
Aluminum foil or colored foil paper, 11-1/2 by 16-1/2 in.
Clear tape
Glue
Christmas cards
Clear, adhesive-backed paper, 12 by 17 in.

Directions:

Cover cardboard backing with aluminum foil or foil paper, turning paper over about 1/2 in. to the back, and secure with clear tape.

Arrange cards in a pleasing design and secure with only enough glue to hold. I would suggest you sort your cards as to design, such as bells, candles, outdoor scenes or color combinations. You may want to use only portions of a card to complete your design. Use only smooth or nearly-smooth cards.

Hold the placemat over the sticky side of the adhesive-backed paper and starting at the top, gently lay the placemat on the paper, making certain it is going together smoothly with no air bubbles. Turn excess adhesive-backed paper to back of the mat, cutting away corners so they lay flat.

A patterned Christmas wrapping paper makes a nice mat itself without the use of cards. Just secure wrap to cardboard with clear tape and cover mat with clear, adhesive-backed paper.

This attractive 3-level candleholder is made of paraffin bars, stacked like bricks. Use the holder all year long or recycle the paraffin.

Paraffin Candleholders: Easy and Economical

By Mary C. Smith
Bellevue, Iowa

IF YOU LIKE pretty things and you like to save money then you'll like these candleholders, especially at Christmastime. And, after the holidays they can be re-cycled. I made these candleholders from eight bars of paraffin (two boxes) for less than a dollar.

Materials:
8 bars paraffin
Small ring mold
11 candles
Greenery, berries, ornaments

Directions:
To make the circular candleholder, melt two or more bars of paraffin in an old black skillet or other suitable old pan. The amount needed for the circular design will depend on the size of your mold. Pour melted paraffin into mold, let it harden and remove by dipping in hot water as in unmolding Jell-O.

Dip the base of each candle in the hot skillet to soften. Hold it a moment

or two on the candleholder until it hardens. Floral "stickum" also works nicely if you don't use too much.

Decorate with a few greens, such as pine or holly and a few red berries or ornaments. I like to use ivy leaves which I always have on hand. If you want to save the circular design for next year, it can be cleaned by rubbing with a piece of nylon hose.

To make the 3-level holder for five candles, stack six bars of paraffin on a thin base to facilitate moving it. Place three bars on the bottom, two in the center and one on the top. The end of each bar is placed in the center of the one below it, like stacking bricks. This makes it simple to place the candles evenly. Attach candles as directed above. Decorate if you wish.

Candles stand on a paraffin ring decorated with ivy, displaying traditional Christmas colors. The ring could also be used for an Advent wreath base (see article on page 2).

43

Lids, Plate, Jars Make Lamp

By Anna May and Anita Yoder
Middlebury, Indiana

THIS LAMP not only makes an attractive Christmas centerpiece, but it can be adapted to complement your everyday decor by exchanging the holiday candle ring for a floral arrangement. The lamp—a conglomeration of parts ranging from jar lids to dinner plates—makes a truly unique centerpiece.

Materials:
Glue (for use on glass, such
*   as Glue-Bird)*
Melmac dinner plate
Vigil Lite candle holder
*   (or small baby food jar)*
Plastic margarine container
*   (1-lb. size, 6-1/4 in. across top)*
Melmac bread and butter plate
*   (edge of plate must match*
*   top of margarine container)*
Screw-type soft drink bottle lid
3-1/4-in. screw-type lid (from 1-lb.
*   Coffee Mate or 27-oz. Tang)*
Hair spray lid (2-1/2 in.)
Glass chimney
8-in. swirl candle
Styrofoam
Candle ring

Directions:
Using Melmac dinner plate for base,
glue each of the parts in order listed above. Place Vigil Lite candle holder or baby food jar upside down and glue on plate. Next, glue plastic margarine container and Melmac bread and butter plate. Glue soft drink bottle lid toward edge of plate. Coffee-Mate lid and hair spray lid should be glued upside down to hold candle.

Spray structure with antique black paint. Then, cut out Styrofoam to hold candle securely inside hair spray lid. Position candle and Styrofoam and cover with glass chimney. Cut candle ring and place at base of lamp.

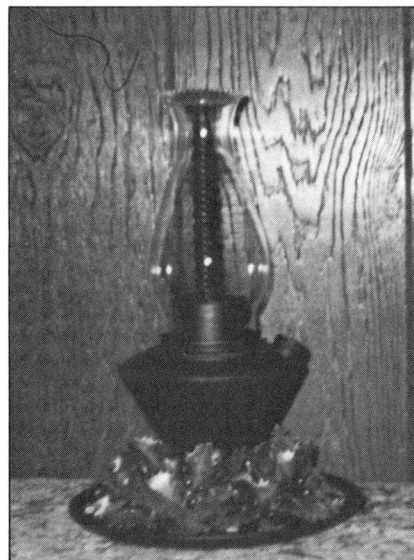

Cheery Candle Perks Up Your Kitchen Table

By Rosellene Keathley Wells
West Point, Mississippi

PERHAPS the most neglected area of the home during Christmas decorating is the kitchen or dining area. Yet, your family table is in constant use. Keeping in mind that you do not want a centerpiece that will crowd your table, you might find that this small table decoration will fit your needs. It's also economical and easy-to-make.

Materials:
Green Styrofoam, at least
*   1 in. thick*
5 stems artificial holly with
*   full-size red berries*
Glass lamp chimney, 8-1/4 in. tall
5- or 6-in. red twisted candle
Small metal candle cup
Red and white checked taffeta bow *

Directions:
Using a sharp knife, cut a 5-in. circle of Styrofoam for the base. Place the chimney in center of base and draw the outline of the bottom of the chimney. With tip of knife, make a shallow groove in Styrofoam to hold chimney.

Chip out a hole about 1/2 in. deep to hold candle cup and insert cup. Put chimney in place.

Lay holly around chimney to form a pleasing circle that hides the stems and covers the base. (Stems are best concealed if holly is placed with stems in alternating directions.) Leave a space in the circle for the bow.

Remove chimney and candle cup while you force holly stems into Styrofoam base to hold them in place.

Anchor bow in place. *You can purchase a ready-made bow of 1-1/2-in.-wide ribbon at the florist or make one yourself as follows: Buy 5 ft. of 1-1/2-in. checked taffeta ribbon. Lay it in soft 5-1/2-in. folds, stacking the lengths as you go. Tie the folds (bow) in center with a fine wire or red thread. Arrange loops in graceful bow. To anchor, attach a short green florist's pick or a round toothpick dipped in green food coloring to the wire or thread at back of bow.

Cut a Carpet For Christmas

IF YOU'RE the kind of hostess who loves to give her Christmas guests the red-carpet treatment—now you can—literally! Choosing carpeting in two contrasting Christmas colors, you can design an area rug for front- and back-door holiday greetings or for a festive fireside family room rug.

Materials:
Textured carpeting
Wide-tipped felt pen
Carpenter's square
Carpet knife
Extra-wide tape

Directions:
To determine exactly how much carpeting you'll need, make a drawing to scale on graph paper (1 square = 1 foot) or have a carpet dealer help you figure the yardage from a diagram.

On the back sides of the two carpet pieces of contrasting colors, transfer the scale proportions. Then, using a wide-tipped felt pen and carpenter's square, draw the design to scale.

Cut sections on the floor from the carpet back, using carpet knife. Then, lay sections on the floor to insure that they will fit properly. Reverse the carpet and tape sections together with extra-wide tape.

To add the finishing touches, cut 5-in.-wide bands of carpet from short ends to achieve a good-looking border effect.

—Courtesy of Armstrong

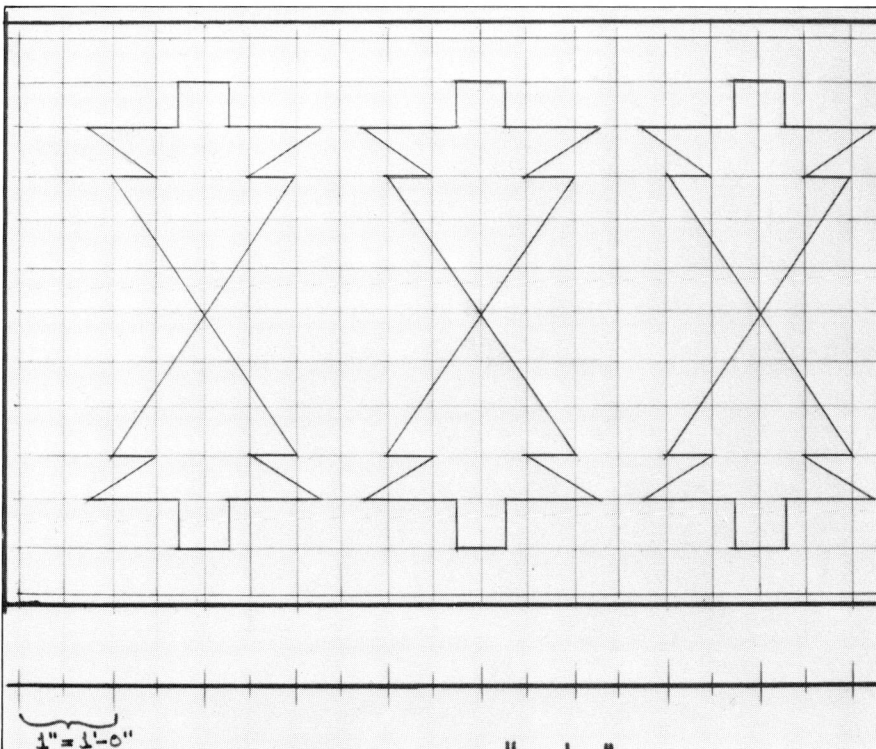

1" = 1'-0"

Set the
Christmas
Scene With . . .   GINGERBREAD!

Directions for gingerbread
tree are on page 48.

Log Cabin Reflects Pioneer Christmas

By Paula Koehler
Jefferson, Wisconsin

A LOG CABIN cookie house is certain to delight the children in your home this Christmas. You can build your log cabin with some cardboard, plywood, tinker toys, construction paper and the ingredients for gingerbread cookies and icing. Boughs and miniature forest creatures may be added.

Materials:

Small cardboard box (1-gal. milk carton works well)
Medium weight cardboard for roof
Large piece of plywood for base, painted green
8 medium tinkertoys
Greenery for landscaping (I used arborvitae leaves)
Small deer, flag, etc. for ornamentation
Construction paper
Food coloring

Gingerbread Cookies:

1-1/2 cup butter or lard
2 cups sugar
4 eggs
2 cups molasses
1 cup sour cream
1 teaspoon salt
4 teaspoons baking soda
2 teaspoons ginger
2 teaspoons cinnamon
12 cups flour

Royal Icing:

2 pounds powdered sugar
1/2 teaspoon cream of tartar
3-4 egg whites

Directions:

Mix together the ingredients for the gingerbread cookies. Pat the cookie dough into greased cookie pans. The dough will fill 4 to 6 pans. Then, using your fingers, pinch the dough together, forming rows in the dough, shaped like horizontal logs. Bake about 15 minutes at 375° till set. Remove carefully and cool.

Meanwhile, combine ingredients for Royal Icing and whip together until stiff. This icing works like glue, so keep it covered with cellophane while using.

Cut the gingerbread cookie the same size as the sides of the box, and attach to box by applying icing. Attach the house bottom to the wooden board with the icing also.

Fold the cardboard for the roof (same length as the house) and slip in between the cardboard box and the cookie walls. Slip four of the tinkertoys underneath for support. Then attach cookie logs to all sides of house and two triangular pieces for the gables. Cut two small pieces of gingerbread for the chimney; glue together, then glue to the top of the house.

To make the porch, cut two pieces the same length as the front of the house, using one piece for the floor and the other for the roof. Cut a piece of cardboard the same size and slip between the roof and the wall of the front of the house. Glue on the roof. Use four tinkertoys for porch posts.

Cut pieces of white construction paper to form windows, and you will need red paper for window boxes. Glue both with icing. Draw flowers, leaves and stems on the walls of the house with decorating tubes.

Place greenery to cover the wood base. Arrange deer, etc. for ornamentation. To make trees, cut different sizes of triangles from construction paper. Roll them into cones, cut the bottoms of the cones even and tape.

Color the remainder of the icing green, and using a leaf tube, make leaves around the cone, starting at the bottom.

No Cutters for These Ginger Men

By Mildred Bienstadt
Milwaukee, Wisconsin

JAUNTY gingerbread men are fun to make and have on hand for family and guests during the holidays. You roll this dough between your hands into balls and logs, then flatten to form the body, head and limbs of the figure. The consistency of the dough makes it easy to work with. You can decorate your gingerbread people in a variety of ways—as snowmen, scarecrows, tramps, Santa, etc.—using confectioners sugar frosting, cloves and miniature chocolate chips. Your children or grandchildren will enjoy helping.

Gingerbread:
2-3/4 cups sifted flour
3 teaspoons baking powder
1/2 teaspoon salt
1 teaspoon ginger
2/3 cup molasses
1/3 cup brown sugar, lightly packed
1 egg
1/3 cup melted butter
Whole cloves

Recipe For a Merry Christmas

Take the crisp cold of December,
Mix with two parts of snow,
Add a dash of fragrant evergreen
And a warm bright candle's glow.

Mix in the warmth of a little girl
The mischief of a small, bright boy,
Stir in slowly the parents' love,
Their wonder and their joy.

Set the mixture to rise with
good will to men
Sprinkle some light from the star,
As it sends the glow as in years ago
When wisemen came from afar.

When it bubbles with warmth and
feeling
Stir with carols, warm and sweet,
This recipe you'll find is sufficient
To serve everyone you meet.

—Kathryn McGaughey
Wheat Ridge, Colorado

Gingerbread figures, above, are made without cutters by flattening balls and logs of dough.

Confectioners Sugar Frosting:
1 tablespoon butter
1/4 cup hot milk
1 teaspoon vanilla
About 3 cups confectioners sugar
Food coloring as desired

Directions:
Mix and sift flour, baking powder, salt and ginger. Combine molasses, brown sugar, well-beaten egg and melted butter; add sifted dry ingredients gradually and mix. Shape into figures. Use clove balls for eyes, stems for nose and mouth. Bake on a greased cookie sheet in preheated 375° oven about 12 minutes.

To mix Confectioners Sugar Frosting, add butter to milk; gradually add sugar to make frosting of the right consistency to spread. Add vanilla. Add food coloring as desired.

Trim a Gingerbread Tree!

A MINIATURE tree made of gingerbread will make a festive centerpiece for the holidays. This Christmas Cookie Tree, pictured on page 46, is pretty, but also crisp, flavorful and easy to make.

Ingredients:
2 14-ounce packages gingerbread mix
3 cups flour
2 teaspoons ground cinnamon
1-1/2 cup butter or margarine
6 tablespoons cold water
48 blanched whole almonds
10-in. Styrofoam cone
Green decorating icing

Directions:
Thoroughly mix first three ingredients; then cut in butter or margarine until like cornmeal. Stir in water; work together on floured board into a smooth ball. Wrap in wax paper and chill.

From cardboard, cut out eleven 8-pointed stars according to pattern on page 109. On floured board, roll out some of dough 1/4 in. thick (use part of it at a time and keep remainder refrigerated). Using cardboard stars, cut out 12 stars (cut out two 2-in. ones). Using 1-3/4-in. round cookie cutter, cut out 9 small rounds. Cut out a 3/4-in. hole in the center of all the rounds and all the stars but the 2-in. ones.

With broad floured spatulas lift stars to greased cookie sheets. Split almonds in half lengthwise. Place one on top of each point of all but the 2-in. stars, pressing them on slightly. For 2-in. stars, cut each of 4 almonds into 4 lengthwise pieces.

Bake stars and rounds in a preheated moderate oven (375° F.) 15 to 20 minutes, or until done. Cool 10 minutes; then remove to rack to cool completely.

To assemble, cut a 1-in. thick base from Styrofoam, leaving a thin long stem in center. Slip largest star down on stem; then slip on a cookie round; then next size star and so on to the 3-in. star. Level stem with cookie. Sandwich the 2-in. stars together with a little icing. Insert on end of a wooden pick between the joined stars. Place on top of tree, inserting the other end of the wooden pick in stem. Garnish points of stars with icing.

—Courtesy of Nabisco, Inc.

Holiday Hints... to make your season

more meaningful, more fun, less hectic

BOUNCING SNOWBALLS: A bowl of bouncing snowballs makes a festive centerpiece. Fasten a candle or china Santa to the bottom of a fish bowl with modeling clay. Fill bowl with water. Add 15 to 20 moth balls, 1 teaspoon citric acid and 1 teaspoon baking soda. This mixture keeps the moth balls bobbing up and down for some time. Add more acid and soda when action stops.

—Mrs. Otto Stank
Pound, Wisconsin

SET TREE FOR BIRDS: Instead of simply throwing out your Christmas tree after the holidays, sink a pail of water in a snowbank near your window and place tree trunk to freeze in it. Watch the birds eat their seeds on it and disappear under the snow-covered boughs.

—Mrs. T.
Iowa

LET MANGER TELL STORY: To help prevent the let-down that sometimes comes after Christmas finally arrives, I usually leave the manger scene up when I take down the tree and other decorations. If you have a scene with separate figures, you can go a step further. Before Christmas, arrange only Mary, Joseph, Jesus and the animals in the stable. Then on Christmas Eve bring the shepherds to the stable. The day after Christmas, place the Wise Men in the room in the house that is farthest from the manger. Each day the small children in the family will delight in helping move the Wise Men one room closer. They should arrive at the stable on January 6, Epiphany. This will also help children realize that there was a span of time between the birth of Christ and the visit of the Wise Men.

—Mrs. Frank Miller
Middlebury, Indiana

FAMILY GIFT EXCHANGE: My family (brothers and sisters and their families) has done several different things for the adult gift exchange at Christmas. One year each person was to make the gift for the person whose name he had drawn. (We even had some men sewing!)

Another year we had a white elephant exchange. It was fun and we found that someone else's trash could indeed be our treasure.

Yet another year we used the money that we would have spent on a gift and gave it to our church relief organization.

Next year both children and adults are planning to take a stocking to hang on the fireplace mantel to be filled with small items by the person who has our name.

Another possibility would be a Loan-It-for-One-Year gift. For example, a book or a record or any other item would be given to the person whose name you had and they could use that item for one year and then return it the following Christmas.

Add a new twist to your gift exchange and you, too, will find that gift giving will take on new meaning.

—Mrs. Frank Miller
Middlebury, Indiana

HOSPITALITY WREATH: On a green Styrofoam wreath form, pin plastic sandwich bags of candy, alternating with red and green bows. Hang on door or use as a table centerpiece. Give filled bags as gifts to visitors.

—Julie Klee
Streator, Illinois

RECYCLE YOUR WREATH: I found a large wreath in our granary (I'd hung it there after Christmas instead of throwing it away) which had housed a nest of baby birds over the summer. I covered the pinecones and nest with plastic sandwich bags and sprayed the old wreath with holly green paint. I left the nest to show. I added a new

red plastic bow and hung the wreath in place. It was really simple and inexpensive—so save your Christmas wreath this year and recycle it!

—Karen Schmidt
Randolph, Wisconsin

MAKE PAPER BOWS: Beautiful bows and decorations for Christmas packages can be made from almost any paper. You can use the same wrapping paper with which the package is being wrapped and thus have a matching bow, or use a contrasting color. All you do is cut narrow strips of the paper and curl it as you do the regular curling ribbon you buy. Almost any paper will curl in this way, and you are only limited by your imagination in the many things you can do with these curls. Even newspaper makes lovely curled bows in this way.

—Tessie McCall
Mesa, Washington

NEW DECORATIONS EACH YEAR: Every year, for the past 10 years, our family has made a completely new set of decorations for our Christmas tree. When the children were about 4 or 5, we made simple things like gingerbread cookies, toothpick Styrofoam balls and painted wood shapes. As they grew older we tried more difficult ones. These included Swedish straw decorations (made with collected Kansas straw), tissue paper origami, white roses with the dove of peace, and milkweed pod birds.

The most time-consuming were the Styrofoam Chrismons we made in 1974. Last year we were leaving on our vacation the day after Christmas so we simply hung beautiful religious cards and white bows

We have stored our decorations each year. Sometimes I've used them in my classroom, and some day we plan a tree using some of each.

—Mrs. Roger Duff
Farmington, Minnesota

Christmas

By Mary E. Allen
Plymouth, New Hampshire

CHRISTMAS Eve is feted in many ways in the various countries around the world. And it's interesting to discover the many customs involving the foods served at that time.

In America, a supper with a steaming pot of oyster stew as the main appetite appeaser is traditional in many homes. During my childhood, this was a special treat of the Christmas season.

The early Pennsylvania Dutch ladies baked special cookies, "by the bushel", to pass out to guests and Christmas Eve trick-or-treaters, who were called Belsnickels.

In England, according to tradition, a special Christmas Bread*—a yeast dough filled with raisins, currants, citron, and spices—must be baked that night. If this is done, the bread will not mold.

And if a slice is left on the table after the Christmas Eve dinner, the family will never want for bread during the coming year.

The Noel Eve feast is served after midnight mass in France. It is a festive affair for which the hostess uses her best china, silver and linen. The rooms and table are decked with candles, greens and flowers.

The Christmas Eve feast in Sweden traditionally has been a Smorgasbord. The menu often includes roast pork or goose and lutefisk—a traditional favorite.

Swedish Christmas Rice Pudding (Risgrynsgrot)* is the traditional dessert for Christmas Eve. Whoever finds a single almond mixed into the pudding supposedly will be married before the next Christmas arrives.

Breaking of the "blessed wafer" began the Christmas Eve meal in old Russia. After each person had received a piece of the wafer, a feast, often dominated by roast pig, followed.

Eleven courses were customarily served in Czechoslovakia on Christmas Eve. The last consisted of a variety of Christmas cookies.

In the Ukraine, the feast contained 12 dishes, representing the 12 apostles. The dish served first was a porridge of wheat and honey, called "kutia".

In Latvia, small pastries filled with meat traditionally were served at the evening meal on Christmas Eve.

True Hungarian tradition called for a large, round, gaily decorated cake set in the center of the table. Then the other foods for the Christmas Eve meal were set around it. Fish and dumplings containing poppy seeds were usually on this menu.

Mexicans served a special salad of fresh fruits and vegetables along with the other dishes at their Christmas Eve feasts. This Ensalada de Noche Buena (Christmas Eve Salad)* was once served only with sugar, but now is accompanied with French dressing or mayonnaise.

ENGLISH CHRISTMAS BREAD

1-1/3 cup boiling water
1/2 cup sugar
2 teaspoons salt
1/2 cup butter or margarine
1/2 teaspoon nutmeg
1 teaspoon caraway seed
1 teaspoon allspice
1/4 cup warm water, 110° to 115°
2 packages dry yeast

Eve Feasting

1 egg, room temperature
5-1/4 to 5-3/4 cups sifted flour
1/2 cup dried currants
1/3 cup dark or white raisins
1/3 cup finely cut citron

Measure the boiling water into a large bowl with the sugar, salt, butter and spices. Add the yeast to the warm water in a small bowl. Let it stand 3 to 5 minutes. Then stir to dissolve. Add the egg.

When the water-sugar mixture has cooled to lukewarm, add half the flour, then the yeast mixture. Beat until smooth. Add half the remaining flour, mixing with spoon or hands. Then blend in the cut-up fruits with more flour until the sides of the bowl are cleaned. The dough will be soft.

Turn the dough out onto a lightly floured board. Knead gently about 50 strokes, or until the dough is smooth. Place the ball of dough, smooth side down, in a greased bowl. Turn once to grease the top. Cover the bowl with waxed paper, then a dry cloth. Let rise in warm place until doubled, or until dent remains when finger is pressed deep into side of dough.

Punch down. Turn onto floured board and divide in two. Shape each half into a round ball and place on opposite corners of a large greased baking sheet. Do not have balls touching. Let rise in warm place until almost doubled.

Bake at 375° for 30 to 40 minutes, or until well browned. Remove to rack and frost lightly with powdered sugar icing. Sprinkle with nuts, if desired. Makes 2 loaves.

SWEDISH CHRISTMAS RICE PUDDING

1 cup rice (do not use converted rice)
2 tablespoons butter
1 cup water
4 cups milk
1/2 teaspoon salt
1/2 cup heavy cream
1 whole blanched almond
Sugar
Cold milk
Cinnamon (optional)

Wash the rice under cold running water. Boil 1 cup water, add rice and 1 tablespoon butter. Cook uncovered over medium heat until the water has disappeared. Stir it often. Add milk and salt to the rice. Then simmer, covered, over the lowest possible heat (or in top of double boiler over boiling water) until the rice is tender and the milk is absorbed.

Remove from heat and stir in the heavy cream and the almond. Place pudding in a serving dish and sprinkle with sugar and cinnamon. Serve with cold milk.

ENSALADA DE NOCHE BUENA

1 head lettuce, shredded
3 cooked beets, sliced
3 red apples, cored and sliced
3 slices pineapple, quartered
2 oranges, peeled and sliced
2 bananas, sliced
1/2 cup roasted peanuts
1/2 cup pomegranate seeds

Spread lettuce on a large platter. Arrange beets and fruit in a symmetrical design, with the colors contrasting. Sprinkle with peanuts and pomegranate seeds. Serve separately with French dressing or mayonnaise.

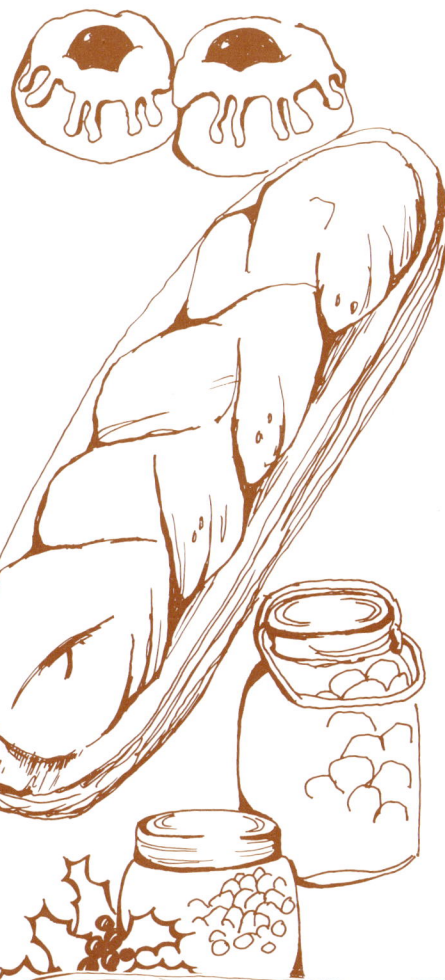

Christmas Brunch Menu

Cheesy Broccoli 'N Ham

or

Eggy-Asparagus Muffs

or

Easy Cheesy Omelet

Fruit Slush   Relishes

Christmas Stollen or Rolls

Black and White Bars   Christmas cookies

Coffee   Tea   Milk

CHEESY BROCCOLI 'N HAM

2 10-ounce packages frozen broccoli in cheese sauce
6 hard-cooked eggs, quartered lengthwise
2 cups ham, diced
1 11-ounce can condensed cheddar cheese soup
1/4 cup milk
1/4 cup butter, melted
1/4 cup water
2 cups herb seasoned stuffing mix

Cook broccoli according to package directions; spread in bottom of 9 x 13-in. pan. Place eggs on broccoli; add ham. Combine soup and milk until smooth; pour over top of broccoli, eggs and ham. Bake at 400° for 15 minutes. Combine butter, water and stuffing mix; sprinkle over casserole. Bake for 15 minutes more. Serves 6 to 8.

*Recipe from
Green Giant Company*

EGGY ASPARAGUS MUFFS

3 English muffins, halved, buttered
1 15-ounce can green asparagus spears, drained
3 hard-cooked eggs, chopped
Salt and pepper
1 can cream of mushroom soup
1/2 cup shredded cheddar cheese
8 slices bacon, diced, fried

Broil buttered muffin halves until golden. Place in 6 individual casseroles or a shallow baking dish. Arrange asparagus spears on each muffin half; top with eggs and sprinkle with salt and pepper. Spoon soup evenly over each muffin. Top with cheese and crisp bacon. Bake at 400° for 15 minutes or until heated through and cheese is melted. Serves 6.

*Recipe from
Green Giant Company*

EASY CHEESY OMELET

8 slices bacon
8 eggs
2/3 cup cream style corn
1 teaspoon salt
1/2 teaspoon pepper
1/2 teaspoon herb seasoning
2/3 cup grated cheese

Pan fry bacon until crisp. Remove, drain and crumble. Beat eggs, add corn and seasonings. Add bacon. Pour slowly into heated skillet which has 2 tablespoons of bacon fat in it. Sprinkle cheese over half the egg mixture. Cook slowly. When eggs begin to set, carefully lift edges with a spatula allowing liquid eggs to run underneath. When top is set, but not dry, carefully fold omelet in half and shake onto a heated platter. Serve immediately. Yield: 6 servings.

*Cathy Peterson
Catawba, Wisconsin*

FRUIT SLUSH

3 medium bananas, mashed
2 oranges, juice and pulp
2 lemons, juice and pulp
1 small can crushed pineapple and juice
1/4 cup maraschino cherries, quartered
1 teaspoon orange rind, grated
1 cup sugar
1 pint ginger ale

Combine ingredients in order given; stir well. Freeze to slush stage, or if made in advance, remove from freezer allowing enough time for fruit to thaw to slush. Serve in sherbet glasses.

*Mrs. Robert Foltz
Shelbyville, Indiana*

BLACK AND WHITE BARS

3/4 cup flour
1/2 cup sugar
1/4 teaspoon baking powder
1/4 teaspoon salt
1 cup oatmeal
1 cup coconut
2/3 cup butter, melted
2 tablespoons cream
2 squares unsweetened baking chocolate
1/3 cup butter
1 cup brown sugar
1 teaspoon vanilla
2 eggs, beaten
2 tablespoons cream
3/4 cup flour
1/2 teaspoon baking powder
1/4 teaspoon salt

Combine first 8 ingredients; blend well. Press into 9 x 13-in. greased pan. Bake at 350° for 12 minutes. Melt the chocolate and butter. Add brown sugar and vanilla. Stir in the eggs and cream; beat well. Stir in the dry ingredients and beat until smooth. Pour over baked crust, return to a 325° oven and bake for 30 minutes. Frost with fudge icing if desired.

*Mrs. Ervin Ocker
Glenvil, Nebraska*

SMELLS OF CHRISTMAS from country kitchens are part of the warmth and joy of the season.

To help in your holiday meal planning, the staff of Farm Wife News put together the menus and recipes on these pages. You may want to try them exactly as given here or substitute some of the other recipes in this book or some of your own favorites, using these menus as guidelines.

So, here's to happy holiday cooking and entertaining!

—Annette Gohlke, Food Editor

Christmas Dinner Menu

Standing Beef Rib Roast

or

Savory Stuffed Pork Shoulder Roast
Sweet-Sour Red Cabbage Slaw

or

Krautomato Casserole
Vegetable Casserole
Potato Cheese Puff
Applesauce Deluxe

or

Fluffy-Topped Pear Salad
Cranberry Holiday Pudding with Vanilla Sauce

or

Eggnog Chiffon Pie
Christmas Cookies
Coffee   Tea   Milk

SAVORY STUFFED PORK SHOULDER ROAST

- 4 to 5-pound pork shoulder roast with pocket for stuffing
- 6 tablespoons butter
- 3/4 cup onion, chopped
- 3/4 cup green pepper, chopped
- 3/4 cup celery, thinly sliced
- 9 Shredded Wheat biscuits, crumbled (5 cups)
- 1 teaspoon poultry seasoning
- 1/4 teaspoon pepper
- 3/4 teaspoon salt
- 1/2 cup chicken broth
- 8-3/4 ounce can whole kernel corn, drained

Saute onion, green pepper and celery in the butter until onion is golden; remove from heat. In large bowl combine the biscuit crumbs and seasonings. Add onion mixture, broth and corn; mix well. Stuff roast with as much stuffing as pocket will hold; secure opening with skewers. Spoon remaining stuffing into a 1-quart casserole, cover loosely with foil and bake for last half hour along with roast. Rub outside of roast with salt. Place on rack in roasting pan. Roast at 350° about 2-1/2 hours or until done. Cover roast with foil if top gets too brown. Serves 8 with an extra 1/3 cup stuffing per person.

Recipe from Nabisco, Inc.

POTATO CHEESE PUFF

- 3 eggs, separated
- 1/4 cup milk
- 3 cups mashed potatoes, seasoned
- 1 teaspoon onion, grated
- 1 tablespoon parsley, chopped
- 2 cups cheese, shredded

Combine egg yolks and milk. Add remaining ingredients, except egg whites; beat well. Beat egg whites stiff; fold into potato mixture. Spoon into a greased 2-quart baking dish. Bake at 375° for 40 to 45 minutes, or until knife inserted in the center comes out clean and the top is browned. Serve immediately. Yield: six 1-cup servings.

Recipe from the USDA

SWEET-SOUR RED CABBAGE SLAW

- 3-pound head red cabbage, shredded
- 4 cooking apples, chopped
- 1/2 cup vegetable oil or lard
- 1 large onion, sliced
- 1/2 cup apple cider vinegar
- 1/4 cup sugar
- Salt and pepper to taste

Saute onion in oil until soft, but not browned. Add vinegar, sugar, salt and pepper. Stir in cabbage and apples and cook over low heat until done, about 20 to 30 minutes. Stir occasionally. Add a tablespoon or two of water if mixture becomes too dry.

Lydia Rittmiller
Fessenden, North Dakota

KRAUTOMATO CASSEROLE

- 1 medium size can tomatoes
- 1 medium size can sauerkraut
- 1 small onion, grated
- 1/8 teaspoon marjoram
- 1 teaspoon brown sugar
- 4 slices toast, cubed
- 4 slices bacon, fried, crumbled

Combine tomatoes, kraut, onion and seasonings. Into a greased casserole, place layers of toast, bacon and kraut mixture. Pour bacon drippings over top. Bake at 350° for about 25 minutes or until top is brown.

Mrs. Verda Ross
San Bernardino, California

VEGETABLE CASSEROLE

- 10-ounce package frozen broccoli
- 10-ounce package frozen cauliflower
- 10-ounce package Brussels sprouts
- 10-ounce package frozen pearl onions in cream sauce*
- 1 can cream of mushroom soup
- 1 small jar Cheese Whiz

*If you cannot find the onions in cream sauce, use 1 can cream of onion soup and plain frozen pearl onions (or canned). Par cook vegetables by just bringing them to a boil. Remove from heat and drain. Combine vegetables in a buttered 2-quart casserole. In a saucepan heat the soups and cheese. Pour over vegetables, top with buttered crumbs and bake at 350° for 45 minutes.

Mrs. Beverly Gust
Durbin, North Dakota

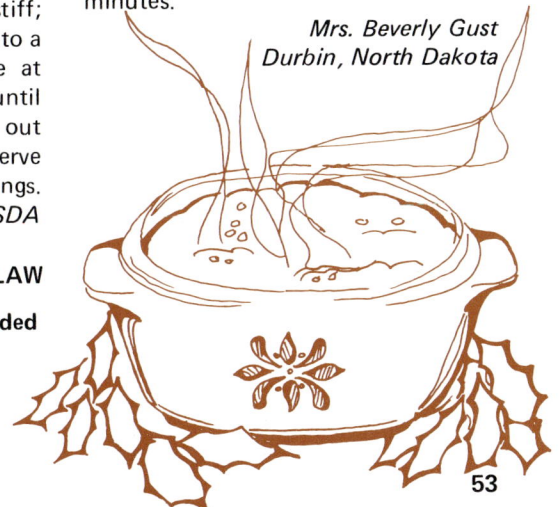

APPLESAUCE DELUXE

3-ounce package raspberry or
  cherry gelatin
1 cup boiling water
1-1/2 cups applesauce
1 teaspoon lemon juice

Dissolve gelatin in boiling water. Blend
in applesauce and lemon juice. Pour
into mold and chill until firm. Serves 4
to 5.

Recipe from the Joys of Jello
General Foods Corp.

FLUFFY-TOPPED PEAR SALAD

1-pound, 13-ounce can pear halves,
  drained
1 cup toasted walnuts, chopped
1/2 cup whipping cream, whipped
1 cup cottage cheese
2 tablespoons confectioners sugar
1 teaspoon orange peel, grated
Dash nutmeg

Gently roll or sprinkle pears with nuts.
Place on lettuce leaf on salad plate.
Combine remaining ingredients and
spoon into pear cavity. Garnish with
orange peel and nuts.

Recipe from
United Dairy Industry Assoc.

CRANBERRY HOLIDAY PUDDING
WITH VANILLA SAUCE

3 cups raw cranberries
3/4 cup seedless white raisins
2-1/4 cups flour
3 teaspoons baking soda
3/4 cup light molasses
1/2 cup hot water

Sauce:
2 cups sugar
1 cup evaporated milk
1 cup butter
2 teaspoons vanilla

Rinse and drain cranberries and raisins. Add flour and soda; stir. Add
molasses and water, blend well. Pour
into greased 9 x 13-in. pan. Cover pan
lightly with foil and bake at 325° for
1 hour. **Sauce:** Combine ingredients
and boil for 5 minutes. Serve over
cranberry pudding. Pudding and sauce
keep well in the refrigerator. Reheat
both to serve.

Susan Lowe
Orland, California

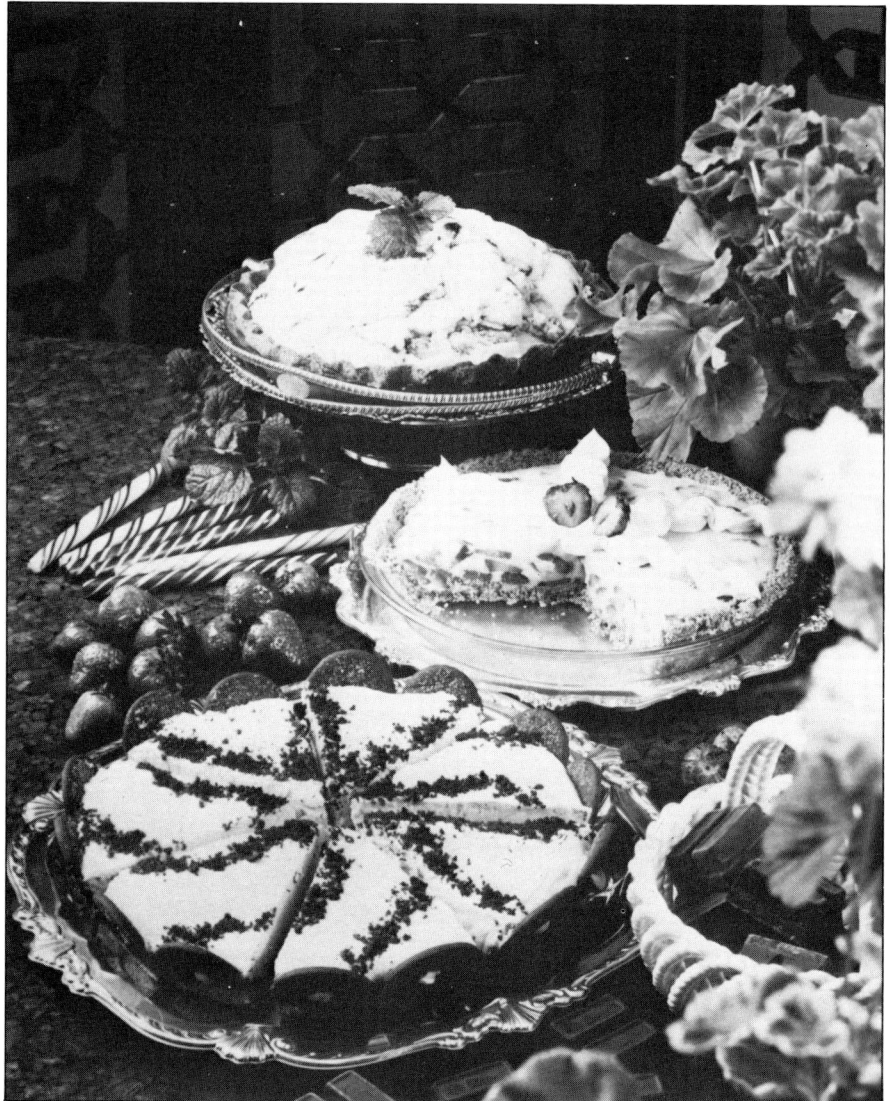

Special desserts are the finale of your holiday meals. Try some of the recipes in this section.

EGGNOG CHIFFON PIE

1-2/3 cups graham cracker crumbs
3/4 cup sugar, divided
1/4 cup butter, softened
1/4 teaspoon nutmeg
4 eggs, separated
1 envelope unflavored gelatin
1/4 teaspoon salt
1-3/4 cup milk, scalded
1/4 cup rum or 1 teaspoon rum
  flavoring
12-ounce jar apricot preserves
1/4 cup orange juice
1 tablespoon lemon juice

Blend the crumbs, 1/4 cup sugar,
butter and nutmeg together. Press
firmly against the bottom and sides of
a 9-in. pie plate. Bake at 375° for 8
minutes. Cool. In double boiler top,
beat egg yolks until thick and creamy.
Combine gelatin and 1/4 cup sugar;
beat into egg yolks. Add salt; then stir
in milk until smooth. Cook over simmering water about 10 minutes until
thickened, stirring constantly. Remove
from heat; cool. Stir in rum. Chill until
mixture mounds when dropped from
spoon. Beat egg whites until soft peaks
form. Gradually add remaining sugar,
beating until stiff. Fold into custard
mixture. Return to refrigerator for 15
minutes. Mound into pie shell. Chill at
least 3 hours until set. Meanwhile heat
apricot preserves with orange and
lemon juices. Drizzle several tablespoons over pie to garnish. Serve remaining sauce warm with pie. Serves 8.

Recipe from Nabisco, Inc.

Holiday Buffet

Ruby Citrus Punch   *Curry Salted Peanuts*

Round Steak Italia

or

Baked Chicken Breasts Supreme

Deviled Eggs   *Zesty Vegetable Salad*

Sorghum Rye Bread

or

Parker House Rolls

Mrs. Betzer's Chocolate Refrigerator Cake

or

Frosty Nesselrode Pudding

Christmas Cookies   *Sweet Breads*

Coffee   *Tea*   *Milk*

RUBY CITRUS PUNCH

- 2 cups orange juice
- 2 cups pineapple juice
- 1/2 cup lemon juice
- 2 quarts raspberry sherbert
- 4 quarts ginger ale, chilled

Combine fruit juices and refrigerate. About 5 minutes before serving, add juices to sherbert and ale. Yield: 30 servings.

Mrs. Albert H. Diercks
Goodhue, Minnesota

CURRY SALTED PEANUTS

- 1 cup salted peanuts
- 1 teaspoon curry powder

Shake the curry powder over the peanuts. Spread on cookie sheet and bake at 300° for 20 minutes, stirring once during baking.

Mrs. Otto Stank
Pound, Wisconsin

ROUND STEAK ITALIA

- 1-1/2 pounds beef round steak, 3/4-in. thick
- 3 tablespoons flour
- 1 teaspoon salt
- 1/2 teaspoon oregano
- 1/4 teaspoon pepper
- 1 tablespoon cooking fat
- 15-1/2 ounces spaghetti sauce with mushrooms
- 9 ounces frozen Italian-style green beans
- 16 ounces canned whole onions, drained

Preheat oven to 375°. Combine flour and spices. Cut meat into 6 pieces. Dredge meat in the flour mixture, shake off excess. Reserve remaining flour, spice mixture. Brown steak in cooking oil. Arrange meat in a 7 x 11-in. baking dish. Heat sauce and reserved flour mixture together until thickened, stirring constantly. Pour over steak, cover and bake for 45 minutes. Add vegetables, cover and bake another 45 minutes. Yield: 6 servings.

DEVILED EGGS

Boiled hard-cooked eggs
Mayonnaise
Salt and pepper to taste
Sweet pickle relish
Mustard
Pimiento stuffed olives
Salted almonds, chopped and toasted

Boil as many eggs as needed. Cool, peel and slice in half lengthwise. Remove yolks carefully and mash or force through a food ricer. Salt and pepper to taste. Use enough mayonnaise and pickle relish to moisten. Add mustard to taste. Spoon egg yolk mixture back into egg white shell. Top with a whole olive, sprinkle with nuts, garnish with sprigs of parsley.

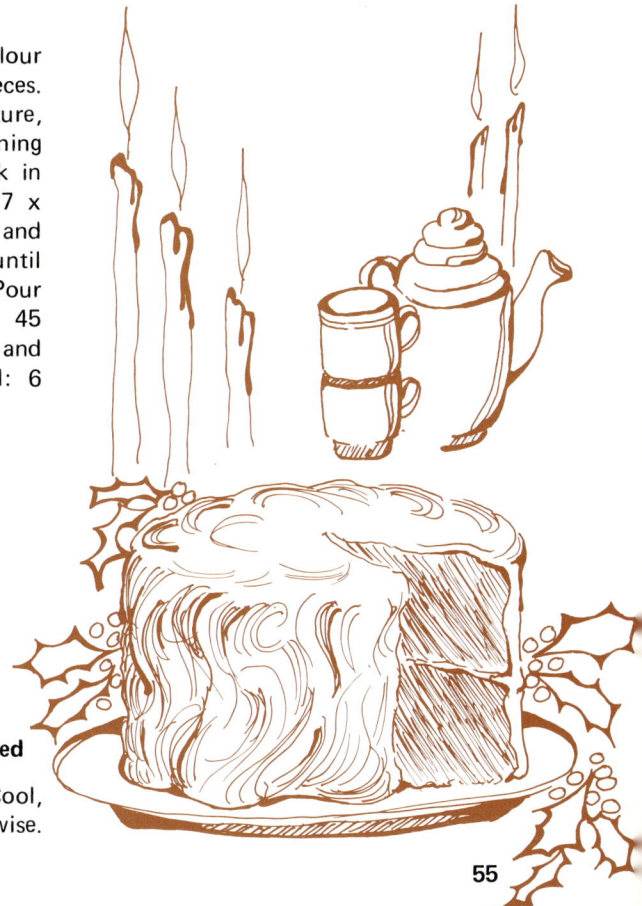

Mrs. Otto Stank
Pound, Wisconsin

ZESTY VEGETABLE SALAD

- 3 medium turnips, pared and sliced
- 3 medium carrots, pared and sliced
- 1/2 small cauliflower, broken into flowers
- 1 small green pepper, cut in strips
- 2 cups water
- 1 teaspoon salt
- 1/2 cup vinegar
- 1/3 cup sugar
- 1/4 cup salad oil
- 2 teaspoons curry powder
- 1 teaspoon salt
- 1/4 teaspoon pepper

Combine vegetables, water and 1 teaspoon salt; bring to a boil, cover and simmer for 5 minutes. Vegetables will be tender, crisp. Drain and cool. Combine remaining ingredients and heat until dissolved. Cool. Pour dressing over vegetables to cover. Refrigerate. This salad keeps for weeks in the refrigerator.

Mrs. Bernard Ausdemore
Crofton, Nebraska

SORGHUM RYE BREAD

2 packages dry yeast
1/2 cup warm water
1/4 cup sorghum
1/3 cup sugar
1 tablespoon salt
1 cup warm water
2 tablespoons shortening
2-1/2 cups rye flour
2-1/2 to 3 cups white flour
1/2 cup raisins or nuts, if desired

Mix yeast and 1/2 cup warm water. Set aside. Combine sorghum, sugar, salt and 1 cup warm water. Add yeast, shortening and rye flour, mix well. Add white flour, nuts or raisins, or both. Knead until dough is smooth and elastic. Let rise in greased bowl, 1-1/2 to 2 hours. Punch down and allow to rise again 30 to 40 minutes. Shape into two loaves in greased pans. Set aside to raise until doubled, 40 to 50 minutes. Bake at 350° 45 to 60 minutes.

Mrs. VaDonna Leaf
Stratford, Iowa

BAKED CHICKEN BREASTS SUPREME

2 cups sour cream
1/4 cup lemon juice
4 teaspoons Worcestershire sauce
2 teaspoons celery salt
2 teaspoons paprika
4 garlic cloves, chopped
4 teaspoons salt
Dash pepper
6 chicken breasts
1-3/4 cup dry bread crumbs
1/2 cup butter

Combine the first 8 ingredients. Skin and bone the chicken breasts and cut in half. Dip the chicken into the sour cream mixture and lay in a shallow pan. Spread the remainder of sauce over chicken; cover and refrigerate overnight. Next day remove chicken from sauce, shake off excess and roll in bread crumbs. Arrange in single layer in a greased, shallow baking dish. Melt butter and drizzle over chicken. Bake at 350° for 45 minutes to 1 hour or until chicken is tender and nicely browned.

Mrs. William Umbarger
Fairfax, Missouri

A festive buffet, a whole meal or just beverage and desserts, makes for great entertaining.

MRS. BETZER'S CHOCOLATE REFRIGERATOR CAKE

1-1/2 pounds vanilla wafers or coconut macaroons
1/2 cup butter, melted
1 pound confectioners sugar
1-1/2 cup butter
5 ounces bitter chocolate, melted
8 eggs, separated
3/4 cup almonds, browned in butter
1 teaspoon vanilla
Whipped cream

Grind or crush the wafers or macaroons into fine crumbs. Add butter, mix well. Press into bottom of a 9 x 13-in. pan. Reserve a few crumbs for garnishing top of torte. Cream together the confectioners sugar, butter, chocolate and egg yolks. Fold in the almonds browned in butter. Beat the egg whites until stiff, but not dry. Fold in vanilla. Gently fold egg whites into chocolate mixture. Spread into crumb-lined pan. Sprinkle with re-served crumbs. Refrigerate 24 hours. Serve with whipped cream, if desired.

Mrs. Frances Betzer
Kenosha, Wisconsin

FROSTY NESSELRODE PUDDING

1-1/2 quarts vanilla ice cream
8 ounces mixed candied fruit, chopped
1/4 cup seedless raisins, chopped
1/4 cup nuts, chopped
1 teaspoon rum extract

Chill a 5 or 6 cup mold. Place ice cream in bowl and refrigerate 15 to 20 minutes to soften. Meanwhile combine fruits, raisins, nuts and extract; toss to blend. Stir ice cream until smooth; fold in fruit mixture. Spoon into mold; freeze. To unmold dip into warm water and turn out onto chilled plate. Yield: 8 to 10 servings.

Recipe from
United Dairy Industry Assoc.

Christmas Calls for Cookies

APRICOT JEWELS

1-1/4 cup flour
1/4 cup sugar
1-1/2 teaspoon baking powder
1/4 teaspoon salt
1/2 cup butter
1 3-ounce package cream cheese
1/2 cup flaked coconut
1/2 cup apricot preserves

Combine flour, sugar, baking powder and salt. Cut butter and cheese into flour mixture. Add coconut and preserves, blend until well mixed. Chill dough. Preheat oven to 350°. Drop dough by teaspoonfuls onto ungreased baking sheets. Bake for about 10 minutes until lightly browned. Cool, ice with frosting made with 1 cup powdered sugar, 1 tablespoon soft butter and 1/4 cup apricot preserves. Decorate top of cookie.

Doris Drach
Saunemin, Illinois

BANANA-PINEAPPLE COOKIES

2-1/4 cups flour
3/4 teaspoon soda
1-1/2 teaspoon salt
1/4 teaspoon nutmeg
1/2 teaspoon cinnamon
3 cups sugar
2-1/2 sticks butter
2 eggs
1-1/2 cups banana, mashed
2-1/2 cups oats
1 cup walnuts, chopped
1 cup crushed pineapple, drained

Preheat oven to 400°. Combine dry ingredients. Cream butter and sugar, add eggs one at a time, beating until light and fluffy. Stir in flour, bananas, oats, nuts and pineapple, blend well. Drop by teaspoonfuls onto lightly greased cookie sheets. Bake about 15 minutes or until lightly browned around edges. Yield: 3 to 4 dozen.

Janet Hollandsworth
Neosho, Missouri

CHOCOLATE SPRITZ COOKIES

3/4 cup butter
1 cup sugar
1 egg, well beaten
1/4 teaspoon salt
2 squares unsweetened chocolate, melted
1/2 teaspoon vanilla
2 tablespoons milk
2 cups flour
Multicolored candy Jimmies

Preheat oven to 375°. Cream butter, sugar and egg until light and fluffy. Add salt, chocolate, milk and vanilla, mix well. Stir in flour, blend well. Shape into small balls, dip tops in decorative candy; place on ungreased baking sheet. Bake 8 to 10 minutes. Dough may be shaped into 1-1/2-in. diameter roll, rolled in decorative candy, chilled; then sliced about ·1/4-in. thick and baked 5 to 8 minutes.

Sara Tatham
Plymouth, New Hampshire

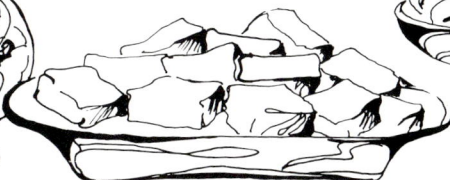

BUMBLEBEES

3/4 cup dates
3/4 cup raisins
1/4 cup candied ginger
3 large dried figs
1/3 cup candied lemon peel
3/4 cup almonds
1/3 cup sweetened condensed milk
1/4 teaspoon vanilla
2/3 cup coconut
Small package of sliced unblanched almonds

Preheat oven to 350°. Put first six ingredients through food chopper using the coarse blade. Add the condensed (*not evaporated*) milk, vanilla and coconut. Shape into ovals the size of an olive. Roll in coconut and stick a slice of almond into each side to resemble the wings of a bumblebee. Place on foil lined cookie sheet and bake 8 to 10 minutes or until coconut is lightly browned. Turn off heat and cool in open oven.

Ruth Hibbs
Statesboro, Georgia

CHERRY FILLED COOKIES:

1/2 cup butter
1 cup sugar
2 eggs
1 teaspoon vanilla
2-1/2 cups flour
1/4 teaspoon soda
1/2 teaspoon salt

Cherry Filling:

    1 cup sugar
    3 tablespoons cornstarch
    1 cup orange juice
    1/2 cup maraschino cherry juice
    24 maraschino cherries, chopped
    2 tablespoons butter

Beat butter, sugar and eggs until light and fluffy. Stir in vanilla. Combine dry ingredients, add to creamed mixture; stir until blended. Chill dough. Preheat oven to 400°. Roll dough on floured board to 1/16-in. thick. Cut with round cutter, or any desired shape, cutting 2 alike for each filled cookie. Bake 8 to 10 minutes. Cool. Spread with cherry filling, top with second cookie. **Cherry Filling:** Combine dry ingredients in saucepan, add remaining ingredients; cook, stirring constantly until thick. Chill. Yield: 2-2/3 cups.

Nancy A. Bender
Coshocton, Ohio

CHEESE CHARMERS

    1/2 cup sugar
    3/4 cup butter
    1/2 cup sharp cheddar cheese, shredded
    1/2 cup thick sweetened applesauce
    2-1/2 cups flour
    1/4 teaspoon salt
    1/4 cup sugar
    1/2 teaspoon cinnamon

Cream sugar and butter, blend in cheese and apple sauce. Add flour and

salt, mix well. Shape into 1-in. balls, roll in sugar, cinnamon mixture and flatten. Bake at 350° for 13 to 16 minutes. Yield: 3 dozen.

Mrs. Vernon E. Zickert
Deerfield, Wisconsin

CHRISTMAS SNOWBALL COOKIES

    1 cup butter
    1/2 cup confectioners sugar
    2 cups flour
    2 teaspoons vanilla
    3/4 cup nuts, chopped

Preheat oven to 350°. Cream butter with sugar, work in flour, vanilla and nuts. Shape into 1-in. balls, place on cookie sheet and bake until light brown. Roll in additional powdered sugar immediately upon removing from oven. Place on rack to cool, then roll once more in sugar.

Mrs. Allen Hanson
Volin, South Dakota

CRANBERRY KITCHEN COOKIES

    1/2 cup butter
    1-1/2 cup sugar
    3/4 cup brown sugar
    1/4 cup milk
    1 egg
    2 tablespoons orange juice
    3 cups flour
    1 teaspoon baking powder
    1/4 teaspoon baking soda
    1/2 teaspoon salt
    1 cup nuts, chopped
    2-1/2 cups fresh cranberries, coarsely chopped

Preheat oven to 375°. Cream butter

and sugars; beat in milk, egg and orange juice. Combine flour, baking powder, soda and salt. Stir into creamed mixture, blend well. Stir in nuts and cranberries. Drop by teaspoonfuls onto greased cookie sheet. Bake 10 to 15 minutes. Yield: 12 dozen tea size cookies.

Regina Nighswander
Leipsic, Ohio

CHRISTMAS ROCKS

    1 cup butter
    1-1/2 cup brown sugar
    2 eggs, beaten
    1 teaspoon cinnamon
    2-1/2 cups flour
    1 teaspoon soda
    1 teaspoon salt
    1-1/2 pound dates
    12 ounces candied cherries, chopped
    12 ounces candied pineapple, chopped
    1-1/4 cup walnuts, chopped
    1/2 pound almonds, blanched and chopped
    1/2 pound Brazil nuts, chopped

Preheat oven to 350°. Cream butter and sugar. Add eggs, beat until light and fluffy. Combine fruit and nuts with 1/2 cup of the flour. Add the remaining 2 cups of flour, cinnamon soda and salt to the creamed mixture. Stir in the fruit and nut mixture by hand until well blended. Roll in balls, dip in sugar and bake for 12 minutes. Baking time will depend on size of

ball. Test 1 cookie first before baking complete batch. Yield: about 12 dozen cookies.

Mrs. Clarence Kramer
Norfolk, Nebraska

FAIRY CAKES

    4 eggs
1-1/2 cup sugar
    1/4 teaspoon anise oil or 1 teaspoon
        anise extract
2-1/2 cups flour

Beat eggs well. Add sugar gradually, beating until light in color. Add flavoring. Gently mix in flour by hand. Drop by teaspoonfuls onto greased cookie sheet. Cookies may be decorated with candied cherries or nuts at this point. Let stand overnight in a cool place. Preheat oven to 350°. Bake 8 to 10 minutes.

Carol Luginbuhl
Roanoke, Illinois

DATE PECAN BALLS

    1 cup butter
    1/2 cup sugar
    2 teaspoons vanilla
2-1/2 cups flour
1-1/2 cup ground pecans
    1 cup dates, chopped
    1/2 cup confectioners sugar

Cream butter, sugar and vanilla. Add flour, mix well. Stir in nuts and dates. Chill 1 hour. Preheat oven to 350°. Roll into small balls. Bake on greased cookie sheet 10 to 12 minutes. Cool, roll in confectioners sugar.

Mrs. Ervin Stahl
Luxemburg, Wisconsin

FILLED COOKIES

    1/2 cup butter
    1 cup sugar
    1 egg
    1 teaspoon grated orange peel
    2 teaspoons vanilla
2-1/2 cups flour
    1 teaspoon baking powder
    1/2 teaspoon soda
1-1/2 teaspoon salt
    1/2 cup dairy sour cream

Filling:
    6 pounds Bartlett pears
    1 pound raisins
Rind of one lemon
Juice of two lemons
    3 to 3-1/2 pounds sugar
    1 20-ounce can crushed
        pineapple, drained
    1/2 teaspoon ginger
    1 teaspoon salt

Cream butter and sugar. Add egg, orange peel and vanilla. Beat until fluffy. Combine dry ingredients, add to creamed mixture alternately with sour cream. Chill dough overnight. **Filling:** Peel and core pears. Grind pears, raisins and lemon peel. Place in heavy kettle with lemon juice, sugar, pineapple, salt and ginger. Simmer until soft and thick, stirring occasionally. Cool. Make this filling in fall. Freeze, remove as needed.

   Roll dough 1/8-in. thick. Cut into 2-3/4-in. circles. Spoon 1-1/2 teaspoon filling onto center of half the cookies. Top with remaining cookies. Bake in 425° oven 8 to 10 minutes until well browned.

Mrs. Paul Grofvert
Kalamazoo, Michigan

GELATIN OATMEAL COOKIES

    1 3-ounce box strawberry or
        raspberry flavored gelatin
3/4 cup sugar
1/2 cup milk
1/8 teaspoon salt
    1 tablespoon light corn syrup
    1 tablespoon butter
3/4 cup quick oats
3/4 cup flake coconut
1/4 cup nuts, chopped

Combine gelatin, sugar, milk, salt and syrup in saucepan. Cook over medium heat, stirring constantly to soft ball stage, 236°. Remove from heat, stir in butter, oatmeal, coconut and nuts. Drop by spoonfuls onto waxed paper. Cool.

Mrs. Eloise Mishler
Clay City, Indiana

GINGER CREAMS

4-1/4 cups flour
    2 teaspoons soda
    2 teaspoons ginger
    1 teaspoon nutmeg
    1 teaspoon cloves
    1 teaspoon cinnamon
    1/2 teaspoon salt
    1/2 cup butter

1 cup sugar
1 egg
1 cup molasses
2/3 cup hot water

Combine the dry ingredients. Cream butter and sugar, add egg; beat well. Add the dry ingredients alternately with the molasses and hot water to the creamed mixture. Chill dough for about 1 hour. Preheat oven to 350°. Drop by rounded teaspoons onto lightly greased baking sheet. Bake 9 to 12 minutes. Cool 1 minute, remove from sheet to wire rack. Frost with creamy vanilla frosting: 2 cups confectioners sugar, 1 teaspoon vanilla, 2 tablespoons soft butter, 1 to 3 tablespoons cream for desired consistency to spread. Combine ingredients and beat well. Yield: 6 dozen.

Mrs. Edmund Prouty
Bryant, South Dakota

GRANDMA'S KRINGLA

1-1/4 cup sugar
1/2 cup shortening
2 eggs
1 cup buttermilk
1 teaspoon soda
3-3/4 cups flour
1 teaspoon baking powder
1/4 teaspoon salt
1 teaspoon vanilla

Mix ingredients as given. Chill dough for several hours or overnight. Remove only a small amount of dough at a time for shaping cookies, (this is the secret to successful Kringlas). Roll small amount of dough into pencil shapes, about 1/4-in. thick. Form into figure 8's as you put onto a cookie sheet. Preheat oven to 350°. Bake about 8 minutes until set, but not brown.

June Reed
Des Moines, Iowa

HUNGARIAN KIFLI

3 cups flour
1 pound butter
1 pound cream cheese

Fillings:*
Prune Butter
Apricot Butter
Raspberry Jam
Nut Filling

Cream butter and cream cheese. Add flour 1 cup at a time. Chill dough overnight. Divide dough into 3 portions. Roll to 1/4-in. thick. Cut dough with crimped wheel or knife into 3-in. squares. Fill with a heaping teaspoon of one of the above fillings. Fold 2 opposite points of square to the center. Bake at 350° for about 10 minutes. Sprinkle with confectioners sugar while still warm. **Prune or Apricot Butter:** Combine 1/2 cup sweetened pureed prunes or apricots, 2 to 4 tablespoons butter, 2 teaspoons grated orange or lemon rind. **Nut Filling:** Combine 2 cups finely ground walnuts, 1 to 2 teaspoons cinnamon, 2 tablespoons sugar and enough water to hold mixture together.

Julia Cunniff
Alstead, New Hampshire

KRIS KRINGLE CHERRIES

1/2 cup butter
1/2 cup brown sugar
1 teaspoon vanilla
1-1/2 cup flour
1/8 teaspoon salt
20 to 25 maraschino cherries
40 to 50 chocolate chips
12 ounces chocolate chips
1-inch piece of paraffin

Preheat oven to 350°. Cream butter and sugar. Add vanilla. Stir in flour and salt, kneading dough slightly if it crumbles. Thoroughly drain the cherries on paper towel. Put 1 or 2 chocolate chips inside each cherry. Wrap 1 teaspoon of dough around each cherry. Bake on ungreased cookie sheet for 15 minutes or until golden brown. Cool; dip in the 12 ounces of chocolate chips melted with paraffin in the top of a double boiler. Place on waxed paper to harden.

Mrs. Allen J. Dornbush
Fulton, Illinois

MARZIPAN COOKIES

1 cup butter, softened
1/2 cup sugar
2-1/2 cups flour
1/2 to 1 teaspoon almond extract
Food coloring

Cream butter and sugar. Stir in flour and almond extract. Work until mixture resembles meal. Divide dough into portions to color. Shape dough into

ORANGE ICEBOX COOKIES

1 cup butter
1/2 cup granulated sugar
1/2 cup brown sugar
1 egg
3 cups flour
1/2 teaspoon salt
1/4 teaspoon soda
Grated rind of 1 orange
2 tablespoons orange juice
1 teaspoon vanilla
1/2 cup toasted almonds, chopped

Cream butter and sugars, beat in egg. Blend in flour, salt and soda. Stir in orange rind, juice, vanilla and nuts. Chill dough until stiff enough to shape into a 1-1/2-in. diameter roll. Chill again. Cut into slices, bake at 375° 12 to 15 minutes. Note: You may freeze the unbaked rolls. Slice frozen dough when ready to bake.

Mrs. Herbert Besthorn
Claflin, Kansas

PINK MERINGUE CLOUDS

Cookie dough:
2 egg yolks
3/4 cup sugar
2/3 cup shortening
1 teaspoon vanilla extract
2-1/2 cups flour
1 teaspoon salt
1/2 teaspoon baking powder
1/4 cup milk

Meringue:
2 egg whites
1/4 teaspoon salt
1/2 cup sugar
1/2 teaspoon vanilla
1/2 teaspoon vinegar
6 ounces chocolate chips

desired fruit shapes, coloring each fruit as directed. Place cookies on ungreased cookie sheets, chill 30 minutes. Bake at 300° about 30 minutes, or until set, but not brown. Baking time will depend upon size and shape of cookies. Yield: about 4 dozen. **Orange dough:** Apricots—shape into small balls, crease. Use clove for stem, brush on diluted red food color for blush. Oranges—shape into small balls, use clove for blossom end. For texture, prick with blunt end of a wooden pick. **Yellow dough:** Bananas—taper and curve 3-in. rolls. Paint on characteristic markings with green or brown food color, (yellow and red make brown). Pears—make pear shapes, use stick cinnamon for stems. Add blush with diluted red food color. **Red dough:** Apples—shape into small balls. Use stick cinnamon for stems. Brush with diluted red food color. Strawberries—make heart shaped fruit. Roll in red sugar. Use green wooden picks for stems. (Lay several wooden tooth picks in green food color for several minutes to dye.) **Green dough:** Peas—make 2-in. flat rounds. Divide level teaspoonfuls of dough into 3 to 4 parts and shape into peas. Place 3 or 4 balls in the center of each round. Bring edges up to form shallow bowl. Green apples—shape as for red apples.

Robbie Uhl
Wilmore, Kansas

1 cup peppermint stick candy, coarsely crushed

Beat egg yolks, sugar and shortening until creamy. Add vanilla. Combine dry ingredients and add alternately with milk to the creamed mixture. Chill dough. Prepare the meringue by beating egg whites and salt in small deep mixing bowl until soft peaks form. Add sugar gradually, beating well until stiff peaks form. Fold in vanilla flavoring, vinegar, chocolate chips and peppermint candy. Shape cookie into a ball using 1 teaspoonful of dough. Place on ungreased cookie sheet. Flatten with bottom of glass dipped in sugar. Top each cookie with a rounded teaspoon of meringue. Bake at 325° 20 to 25 minutes.

Mrs. Darrell Braun
Meadow Grove, Nebraska

SKILLET COOKIES

1/2 cup butter
1 cup sugar
1 egg, beaten
1 cup dates, finely cut
3 cups Rice Krispie cereal
1 cup nuts, chopped
1 teaspoon vanilla
Flaked coconut

Melt butter in large skillet. Add sugar, stir well. Remove from heat. Add egg and dates, stir until blended. Return to heat, cook 5 to 6 minutes. Remove from stove, add remaining ingredients, except coconut. When mixture cools

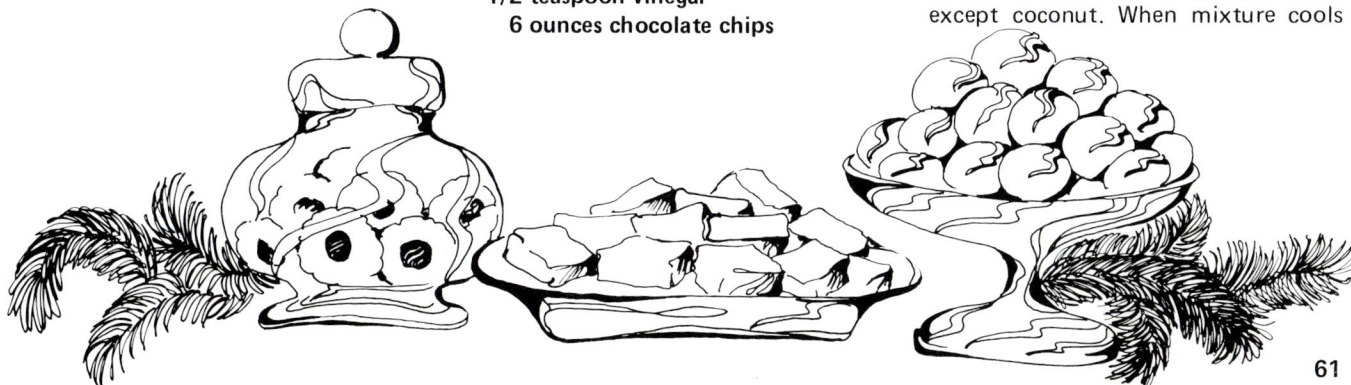

enough to handle, roll into balls of desired size, roll in coconut and place on tray to cool.

Mrs. James A. Waters
Norborne, Missouri

SOUR CREAM PECAN COOKIES

3/4 cup butter
1 cup brown sugar
1/2 cup white sugar
2 eggs
1 tablespoon lemon or orange rind
1/2 cup sour cream
3 cups flour
2 teaspoons baking powder
1/2 teaspoon soda
1/2 teaspoon salt
1 cup pecans, chopped

Preheat oven to 375°. Cream butter, add sugars; cream well. Add eggs, one at a time, beating well after each addition. Stir in sour cream. Combine dry ingredients, add to creamed mixture and blend well. Drop by teaspoonfuls onto lightly greased cookie sheets. Bake 10 to 14 minutes. Cool. Ice with Orange Frosting: 2 cups powdered sugar, 2 teaspoons orange rind, dash of salt, 2 to 3 tablespoons lemon or orange juice.

Mrs. Richard McGlachlin
Sedgwick, Kansas

SPECULAAS

1 cup butter
1-1/2 cup brown sugar
2 to 3 tablespoons milk
3 cups flour
4 teaspoons baking powder
1 tablespoon cinnamon
1 teaspoon cloves
1 teaspoon nutmeg
1/2 teaspoon anise seed
1/4 teaspoon ginger
Dash salt, pepper

Cream butter and sugar, blend in milk. Combine dry ingredients and stir into creamed mixture. Knead dough until smooth. Roll dough and cut into desired shapes, such as diamonds; or divide dough into 2 portions and shape into rolls 1-1/2-in. in diameter. Chill rolls overnight. Slice 1/4-in. thick. Bake at 375° 12 to 15 minutes.

Arlene Brekke
Minneapolis, Minnesota

SPICED ALMOND CAKES

2 cups flour
1 cup sugar
2 teaspoons baking powder
1 teaspoon each nutmeg and cinnamon
1/2 teaspoon each, allspice and cloves
1 cup butter
1 cup ground almonds
2 eggs, separated
Almond slices

Combine dry ingredients, add butter; blend as for pie crust. Stir in almonds. Add egg whites, work into a ball. Chill dough several hours or overnight. Divide dough into 4 portions. Roll on floured board to 1/8-in. thick. Cut into 2-in. circles. Place on greased cookie sheet. Brush with beaten egg yolk and top with almond slice. Bake at 325° for about 10 minutes, or until light brown.

Jeanette Wiederkehr
Waverly, Kansas

SPICED CHERRY BELLS

1 cup butter
1-1/4 cup brown sugar
1/4 cup dark corn syrup
1 tablespoon cream
1 egg
3 cups flour
1/2 teaspoon soda
1/2 teaspoon salt
1 teaspoon ginger
1/2 teaspoon instant coffee

Filling:
1/3 cup brown sugar
1 tablespoon butter
3 tablespoons maraschino cherry juice
1 cup nuts, finely chopped or ground

Cream butter, sugar, syrup, cream and egg until light and fluffy. Add dry ingredients, mix well. Chill dough for easier rolling. **Filling:** Combine ingredients, heat to blend. Cool.

Roll dough about 1/4-in. thick. Cut circle of dough about 2-in. in size. Spoon 1 teaspoon filling on center of each circle. Fold top sides over to resemble bells. Put 1/2 maraschino cherry in center for clapper. Bake at 350° 12 to 25 minutes.

Mrs. Dale H. Fletcher
Mitchell, Indiana

STRAWBERRY DELIGHT COOKIES

1-1/4 cup flour
1/4 cup sugar
1-1/2 teaspoon baking powder
1/4 teaspoon salt
1/2 cup butter
1/3 cup cream cheese
1/2 cup flaked coconut
1/2 cup strawberry preserves

Preheat oven to 350°. Combine flour, sugar, baking powder and salt. Cut in butter and cream cheese. Blend in coconut and preserves. Drop by teaspoonfuls onto cookie sheet. Bake for 15 minutes or until lightly browned. Cool and frost with a blend of 1 cup confectioners sugar, 1 tablespoon soft butter, 1/4 cup strawberry preserves.

Mrs. Keith Wilson
DeSmet, Idaho

TRIPLET COOKIES

Cookie dough:
1 cup brown sugar
1 cup granulated sugar
1 cup butter
2 eggs
2-1/2 cups flour
1 teaspoon salt
1 teaspoon soda

Chocolate Crinkles:
1/3 cup chocolate chips
1/2 cup confectioners sugar

Cherry Almond Drops
1/2 cup maraschino cherries, chopped
1/2 cup coconut, flaked or shredded
1/4 teaspoon almond extract

Date Nut Chews:
1/2 cup dates, cut
1/2 cup nuts chopped

Preheat oven to 350°. Cream sugars, butter and eggs until light and fluffy. Add dry ingredients, mix well. Divide dough into 3 portions. **Chocolate Crinkles:** Melt chocolate, add to 1/3 portion of dough. Shape into 1-in. balls. Roll in confectioners sugar. Place on cookie sheet and bake as directed. Add ingredients of other cookies listed above to 1 of each portion of dough. Drop by teaspoonfuls onto lightly greased cookie sheets. Bake for 15 to 18 minutes. Yield: 6-7 dozen.

Florence Neuendorf
Iowa Falls, Iowa

Sweet Dough Delights for the Holidays

APPLE-TAFFY ROLLS

1 package dry yeast
1/2 cup warm water
1/3 cup sugar
1/3 cup butter
2 teaspoons salt
1 cup milk, scalded
2 eggs
4 to 4-1/2 cups flour
2 tablespoons butter, softened
1 cup thick apple butter
1 cup raisins
1/3 cup dark syrup
2/3 cup brown sugar
1/3 cup butter, melted
1 cup nuts, chopped

Soften yeast in warm water. Blend sugar, butter and salt into hot milk. Cool to lukewarm. Stir in yeast, eggs and 1 cup flour. Beat at medium speed. By hand, stir in remainder of flour. Turn onto floured board and roll out dough. Spread with softened apple butter and raisins. Roll jelly-roll fashion. Using a piece of white thread, cut into 1-in. slices and place on top of the syrup, brown sugar, butter and nut mixture which you have melted in the bottom of a 9 x 13-in. pan. Bake at 400° 15 to 20 minutes or until done.

Mrs. Wayne R. Ebsen
Beresford, South Dakota

APPLE-NUT COFFEE CAKE

1/2 cup butter
1 cup sugar
2 eggs
1 teaspoon vanilla
2 cups flour
1 teaspoon baking powder
1 teaspoon baking soda
1/4 teaspoon salt
1 cup dairy sour cream
2 cups apples, finely chopped

Topping:
1/2 cup nuts, chopped
1/2 cup brown sugar
1 teaspoon cinnamon
2 tablespoons butter

Preheat oven to 350°. Cream butter and sugar, add eggs one at a time, beating well after each addition. Add vanilla. Sift together the flour, baking powder, baking soda and salt. Add to creamed mixture alternately with the sour cream. Fold in apples. Spread batter in a greased 9 x 13-in. pan. Combine topping ingredients and sprinkle over top of cake. Bake for 25 to 40 minutes.

Mrs. Floyd Nicewanner
Stockton, Iowa

APPLE PIE DOUGHNUTS

2 packages dry yeast
1/2 cup warm water
3/4 cup milk, scalded
1/3 cup shortening
1/2 cup sugar
1 teaspoon salt
2 eggs
4-1/2 cups flour
1/2 teaspoon cinnamon
1/2 teaspoon nutmeg

Filling:
1-1/4 cup canned apple slices
1/2 cup brown sugar
1/2 teaspoon salt
1/2 teaspoon cinnamon
1/2 teaspoon nutmeg
1-1/2 teaspoon cornstarch
2 tablespoons water

Soften yeast in warm water. Combine next 4 ingredients, stir until shortening melts and sugar dissolves. Cool. Add yeast and eggs, beat well. Sift flour with spices. Add 2 cups to yeast mixture and beat until very smooth.

Add remaining flour to make a soft dough. Turn onto floured board, knead about 10 minutes until smooth and satiny. Shape into ball, place in greased bowl, turn to grease top. Cover and let rise until doubled in bulk, about 1 hour. Using 1/2 of dough at a time, roll out 1-in. thick and cut into 3-in. rounds. **Filling:** Combine ingredients and cook over low heat until thick. Cool before filling doughnuts. Place a large tablespoon of filling in center of doughnut, fold over and seal edges. Then shape into a ball. Place on greased baking sheet, creased side down. Cover and let rise 20 minutes. Fry in deep fat at 375° until doughnuts are golden brown. When slightly cooled, roll in granulated sugar. Note: Canned apple pie filling, thick apple butter or jam can be used as filling. Nuts may be added if desired.

Mrs. Joyce Uglow
Watertown, Wisconsin

GLAZED RAISED DOUGHNUTS

1 cup potatoes, cooked and mashed
1/3 cup butter
1/2 cup sugar
1-1/2 cup milk, scalded
2 eggs, beaten
2 packages dry yeast
1/3 cup lukewarm water
5 cups flour
1 teaspoon salt

Glaze:
1-1/2 box powdered sugar
2 tablespoons cornstarch
1/4 cup butter, melted
2 tablespoons sweet corn syrup
2 teaspoons vanilla
1/2 cup hot water

Combine potatoes, butter, sugar and milk in mixing bowl and cool to

lukewarm. Add eggs. Dissolve yeast in the warm water, add to cooled milk mixture. Gradually add flour and salt, beat in thoroughly. Turn onto floured board and knead until smooth and elastic. Place in greased bowl, cover and let rise 1 hour. Punch down and let rise 1 hour again, or until double in bulk. Roll out 1/2-in. thick. Cut into round doughnuts, without the hole. Let rise until double in size, about 1/2 hour. Heat lard or oil in deep fryer to 375°. Before you drop into oil, make a hole in the center of the doughnut with your finger. Fry and drain. While still warm, dip in Glaze and cool on cake rack. Yield: 5 dozen.

Mrs. James Williams
Clay Center, Kansas

CUPID'S CHRISTMAS BREAD

    1 package dry yeast
1/2 cup lukewarm water
1/3 cup shortening
1/3 cup brown sugar
    2 teaspoons salt
    1 cup scalded milk
    4 to 4-1/2 cups flour
    1 egg, beaten
    1 cup quick oatmeal
1/2 cup nuts, chopped
    1 cup mixed candied fruit

Soften yeast in lukewarm water. Add shortening, sugar and salt to milk. Cool to lukewarm. Stir in 1 cup of flour. Add egg and yeast. Fold in oats, nuts and fruit. Stir in 3 cups flour to make soft dough. Turn onto floured board and knead, using remaining 1/2 cup flour, until smooth and elastic, about 10 minutes. Place in warm, greased bowl; cover and let rise in warm place until doubled in size, about 1 hour. Punch down. Cover and let rest 10 minutes. Shape into 2 round loaves. Place on greased baking sheet. Brush lightly with melted shortening. Cover and let rise until doubled, about 45 minutes. Bake at 375° for 10 minutes, reduce oven heat to 350°, bake 20 minutes more. Frost with butter icing and decorate.

Mrs. Howard G. Drake
Newfane, New York

PEAR BREAD

    *Basic dough for 4 loaves of bread:
    **1-ounce <u>fresh</u> yeast

    3 tablespoons sugar
3-3/4 cups lukewarm water
    12 cups flour
    1 tablespoon salt

Fruit filling:
    16 ounces dried pears
    3 cups raisins
    1 cup prunes
    8 ounces dried peaches
    8 ounces dried apricots
    8 ounces dried apples
    1 cup English walnuts
    1 cup Black walnuts
    3/4 cup wine
    1/4 cup orange juice
    3/4 cup sugar
1-1/2 teaspoon cinnamon
    3/4 teaspoon allspice
    3/4 teaspoon nutmeg

This recipe calls for enough bread dough to make 4 loaves of bread. You may use your own favorite recipe, or the one printed above. The sugar in the above recipe was increased by 2 tablespoons to make the dough sweeter for this Pear Bread.

**Here is a conversion for <u>fresh</u> yeast to <u>activated</u> <u>dry</u> yeast: 1 ounce of fresh yeast = 1/2 ounce of dried yeast.*

The night before you plan to bake the Pear Bread, chop fruits and nuts for filling and soak in the wine, orange juice and sugar overnight.

On day of baking, crumble the yeast into a small bowl and mash in 1 teaspoon sugar. Add 4 teaspoons water and cream together to make a smooth paste. Set the yeast aside for 15 to 20 minutes until frothy. Put the flour, sugar and salt into a large warm bowl. Make a well in the center of the flour and pour in the yeast and remaining lukewarm water. Draw the flour into the liquid by stirring with a wooden spoon until all the flour is moistened and dough pulls away from the sides of the bowl. Turn onto a floured board and knead for about 10 minutes, reflouring the surface if the dough becomes sticky. Shape dough into a ball and place into a greased bowl. Dust top of dough with a little flour, cover and leave to rise in a warm place until doubled, about 1-1/2 hours. Divide dough into 4 pieces. Set 1 portion aside in a cool place. This is the portion used to wrap the Pear Bread for final baking.

Add the spices to fruit filling mixture. Mix the fruit filling into the 3 portions of dough. Place in lightly greased bowl, cover and let rise until doubled. Divide into 3 portions and shape into loaves. Now take the reserved portion of plain dough, divide it into 3 pieces and roll each out very thin. Wrap around pear loaves. This prevents the fruit from burning as it bakes. Place each loaf into 9 x 5 x 3-in. greased pans. Let rise until almost doubled. Bake at 350° for 1 hour and 15 minutes or until done. Brush tops with butter, frost with butter icing and decorate, if desired.

Mrs. Sharon Fimian
Alma, Wisconsin

HOSKA

    1 cup milk, scalded
1/2 cup butter
3/4 cup sugar
    1 teaspoon salt
    1 teaspoon lemon rind, grated
    2 packages dry yeast
1/2 cup warm water
4-1/2 to 5 cups flour
    1 cup raisins
    2 eggs
Poppy seeds

Combine milk, butter, sugar, salt and lemon rind. Dissolve yeast in warm water, stir into above mixture. Add 2 cups flour, raisins and eggs; beat well. Stir in 2-1/2 cups flour to make soft dough. Turn onto floured board (using 1/2 cup flour) knead until smooth. Place in greased bowl. Turn over once. Cover and let rise in warm place until double. Divide dough in 2 portions. Divide each portion into 4 equal parts. Shape 3 of these parts into strands 14 inches long. Place on lightly greased baking sheet; braid loosely, fastening strands at one end, then tuck under. Divide remaining portion of dough

into 3 parts and shape into 3 strands each 12 inches long. Braid and place on top of first braid. Repeat with other half of dough, to make 2 large braided breads. Cover and let rise until double. Brush with egg yolk mixed with 2 tablespoons water. Sprinkle with poppy seed. Bake at 350° for 30 to 40 minutes until rich brown.

Mrs. Paul Anderson
Hills, Minnesota

STUFFED POTATO BREAD

    1 envelope dry yeast
    1/4 cup warm water
    1/3 cup butter, softened
    2 tablespoons sugar
1-1/2 teaspoons salt
    1/2 cup mashed potato flakes
    1/2 cup hot water
    1/2 cup milk
        1 egg
        4 cups flour

Filling:
    1/3 cup butter
    1/2 cup onion, finely chopped
    1/2 cup celery, finely chopped
        1 tablespoon parsley, minced
        1 teaspoon poultry seasoning
    1/3 cup herb seasoned stuffing mix, crushed fine
    1/2 teaspoon salt

Dissolve yeast in 1/4 cup warm water. In large mixer bowl combine butter, sugar, salt, potato flakes, hot water, milk, egg, yeast and 2 cups flour. Blend at low speed, then beat 3 minutes on medium speed. Stir in remaining flour by hand to form a soft dough. Cover and let rise in warm place till light and doubled in size, 45 to 60 minutes. **Filling:** Melt butter and combine with remaining filling ingredients. Stir dough down, knead on floured board till satiny. Divide in half and roll each piece to an 8 x 12-in. rectangle. Spread each rectangle with half the filling and roll up jelly-roll fashion, sealing ends and seam. Place seam side down in well greased 9 x 5 x 3-in. loaf pans. Let rise till almost double, about 30 to 45 minutes. Bake at 350° for 30 minutes till golden brown. Serve warm.

Mrs. Theodore H. Eckroth
Bloomsburg, Pennsylvania

SUNNY-HONEY PRUNE BREAD

1/2 cup sunflower seeds
    1 cup cooked prunes, chopped
3/4 cup prune liquid
    1 package dry yeast
1/4 cup warm water
    1 cup milk, scalded
    1 tablespoon salt
    4 tablespoons honey
1/4 cup butter
1/4 cup all-bran or bran buds
    6 cups all-purpose flour

Combine *half* the sunflower seeds and prunes. Soften yeast in warm water. Add scalded milk to combined prune liquid, salt, honey, butter; cool to lukewarm. Add bran, mix well. Add 2 cups flour, beat until smooth. Add yeast and prune-sunflower mixture, mix well. Add remaining flour to make soft dough. Knead in bowl until smooth, about 10 minutes. Grease top, turn over in bowl and grease top again. Cover, let rise in warm place 2 hours or until doubled. Turn out, divide in half; let rest 10 minutes. Shape into 2 loaves and place in greased 9 x 5 x 3-in. loaf pans. Brush tops with about 1 tablespoon honey diluted with few drops water. Sprinkle remaining 1/4 cup sunflower seeds over top. Let rise 50-55 minutes. Bake at 375° 40 to 45 minutes. Turn out of pans immediately. Cool on wire rack.

Mrs. Roland Rooney
Buffalo, Minnesota

GRANDMA GEHLBACH'S FRUIT BREAD

1-1/2 cup warm water (105 to 110° F.)
    2 tablespoons sugar
    1 package dry yeast
    7 cups flour
    1 cup milk, scalded
1/2 cup shortening, melted
1/2 cup sugar
    1 egg, well beaten
    1 tablespoon salt
    1 cup raisins
1/2 cup prunes, cooked, chopped
1/2 cup nuts, chopped

Combine water and sugar in large mixing bowl. Sprinkle in yeast, stir until dissolved. Add 2 cups flour, beating until smooth. Cover; let rise in warm place until dough is light, bubbly and spongelike, about 1 hour. Stir sponge down. Combine milk, shortening, sugar, egg and salt. Blend into sponge. Add raisins, prunes and nuts. Stir in enough flour to make a stiff dough. Turn onto floured board, knead until smooth and elastic. Place in greased bowl, turning once to grease top. Cover, let rise in warm place until double in bulk. Punch down and divide into 2 loaves. Place in greased 9 x 5 x 3-in. loaf pans. Cover, let rise until double in bulk. Bake at 350° for about 50 minutes or until done.

Mrs. Harold Dowse
Mason City, Nebraska

POTECA (PO-TEET-ZA)

Basic Sweet Dough:
4-1/2 to 4-3/4 cups flour
    1/2 cup warm water
        2 packages dry yeast
    3/4 cup lukewarm milk
    1/4 cup sugar
        1 teaspoon salt
    1/3 cup shortening
        2 eggs

Filling:
        2 cups graham or vanilla wafer crumbs
        3 cups ground nutmeats
        2 cups brown sugar or 1-1/2 cup brown and 1/2 cup white sugar
        1 teaspoon cinnamon
        1 pound butter, melted
        3 to 4 eggs

Soak yeast in the warm water for 5 minutes. Combine milk, sugar and salt in bowl. Beat in shortening, eggs, yeast mixture and 1 cup flour until smooth. Add remaining flour until dough leaves sides of bowl. Turn out onto floured board. Knead until dough is smooth, elastic and no longer sticky. Place in lightly greased bowl. Cover and let rise

(Continued on page 66)

until doubled in bulk. Punch down. Divide dough in half. Roll dough on floured surface as thin as possible.
Filling : Grind the crumbs and nutmeats very fine. Cream the filling ingredients together. Add cream, if needed, to make filling spreadable. Note: Mrs. Laban writes that she doubles the filling recipe, using a whole recipe for each Poteca. If you prefer to make only one Poteca, divide the Basic Sweet Dough recipe in half. Spread filling on dough. Cut off edges to square off dough. Roll up as tightly as you can. Place in tube or bundt pan, sealing ends together. Repeat with remaining half of dough. Bake immediately without letting Poteca raise a second time. Bake at 375° until lightly browned.

Mrs. Joe Laban
Bernard, Iowa

"HUTZEBROAD"

15 ounces dried apricots, chopped
4 ounces dried prunes, chopped
1/4 cup sugar
1 cup milk, scalded
1/4 cup sour cream
3/4 cup potatoes, mashed
1 cup potato water
1/3 teaspoon baking soda
1/2 cup shortening
1/4 cup dark molasses
2 teaspoons salt
3 packages dry yeast
2 small eggs
3/4 cup dark brown sugar
1/2 cup granulated sugar
2 cups raisins
1 cup nuts, chopped
3/4 teaspoon cinnamon
1/3 teaspoon cloves
1/4 teaspoon nutmeg
8 to 9 cups flour

Combine apricots, prunes and 1/4 cup sugar, set aside. In a large saucepan, combine the next 8 ingredients, heat to lukewarm. Stir in the yeast, eggs and sugars. Combine the apricot-prune mixture with the raisins, nuts, cinnamon, cloves and nutmeg. Stir into the yeast mixture. Pour into a large bowl and add flour, several cups at a time, stirring to make a dough stiff enough to knead. Turn onto a floured board and knead until smooth, about 10 minutes. Place into greased bowl, turning once to grease top. Cover and let rise in warm place until double in bulk. Divide dough into 3 portions, shape into loaves and place in 9 x 5 x 3-in. pans. Let rise until double. Bake at 325° for 50 minutes or until bread sounds hollow when you tap it with your knuckle. Remove from pans immediately, brush tops with butter.

Mrs. Alvin Beutel
Tremont, Illinois

DANISH KRINGLE

2 cups flour
1-1/2 tablespoons sugar
1/2 teaspoon salt
2 tablespoons butter
1 package dry yeast
1/4 cup warm water
1 egg, separated
1/2 cup milk, scalded
1/2 cup butter, softened

Pecan Filling:
1/4 cup butter
1/2 cup brown sugar
1 cup pecans, chopped

Apple Filling:
1/2 cup brown sugar
1 cup apples, finely chopped
1/2 cup pecans, chopped

Date-Pecan Filling:
1/2 cup brown sugar
1 cup dates, finely chopped
1/2 cup pecans, finely chopped

Other Fillings:
Solo Brand prepared fillings, such as, apricot, prune, cherry, poppy seed.

Combine the flour, sugar and salt. Cut in 2 tablespoons butter. Dissolve yeast in warm water. Stir egg yolk into slightly cooled milk. Add milk and yeast to dry ingredients. Beat till well blended. Dough will be soft. Cover and refrigerate 1/2 hour or more. Roll dough into 1/4-in. thick rectangle. Spread 2/3 of surface of dough with a thin layer of the softened butter not quite to the edge of rectangle. Fold the unbuttered 1/3 over the center third. Then fold the remaining 1/3 over the doubled portion. The dough is now in 3 layers. Turn the dough a quarter turn and roll it again into a 1/4-in. thick rectangle. Now repeat buttering and rolling of dough 2 more times. Chill for 2 or more hours.

Prepare filling. To form into Kringles, divide dough in half, return one half to refrigerator. Beat egg white. On a floured board, or pastry cloth sprinkled with flour, roll dough into a 6 x 18-in. rectangle. Spread a 3-in. strip across the center with beaten egg white; then with filling. Fold over one side of dough, then the other side, forming a 1-1/2-in. overlap. Pinch to seal. Arrange in oval or horseshoe shape on well greased pan. Shape and fill second kringle. Cover and let rise in warm place 30 to 45 minutes (dough should no longer be cold.)

Bake at 400° for 20 to 30 minutes until golden brown. Spread with sugar icing while hot. Decorate with whole nuts and cherries.

Edie Van Vleet
Hartland, Wisconsin

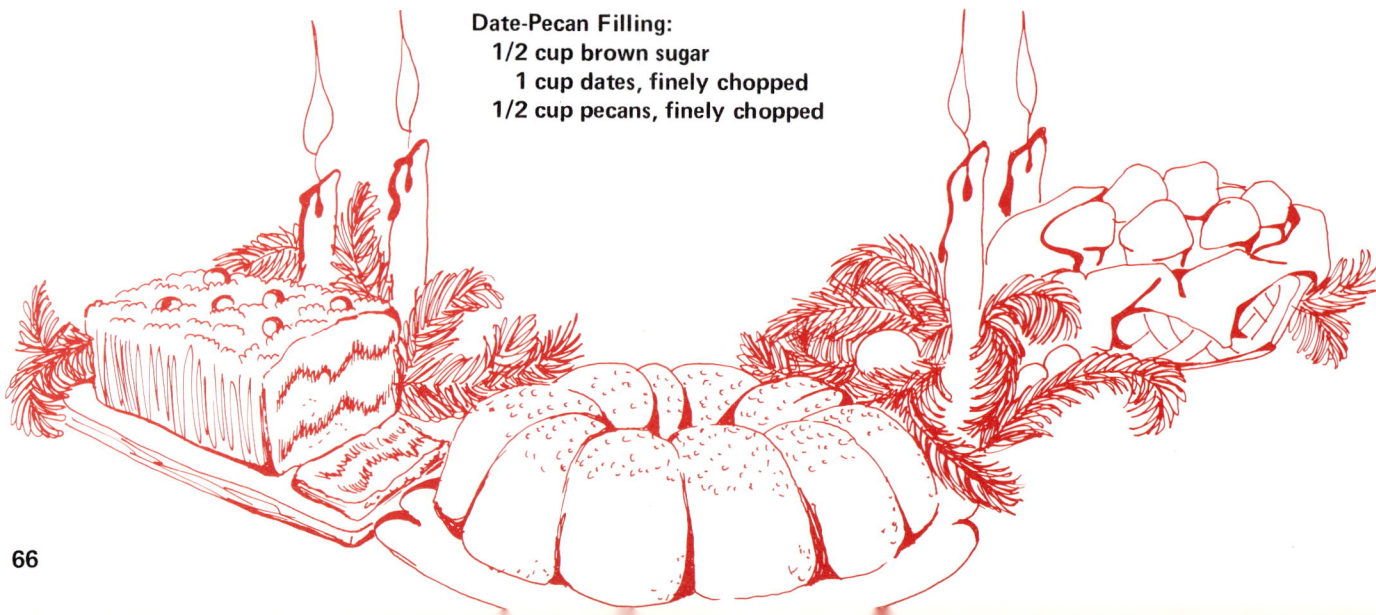

Candies for Christmas

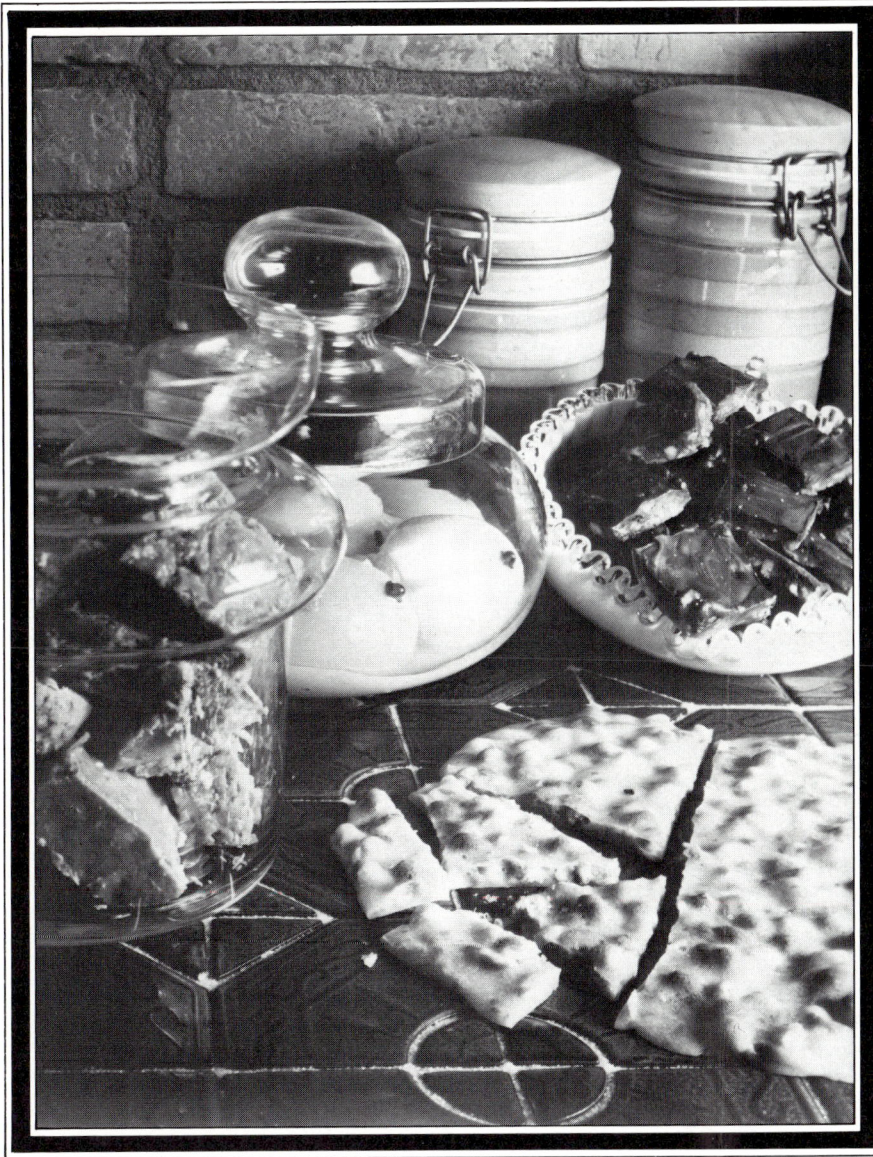

OR condensed milk
3/4 teaspoon vanilla
1/2 cup chopped nuts
2 squares baking chocolate
1/2 cup chocolate chips
2 tablespoons butter
2-in. square paraffin

Combine the first 5 ingredients and shape into balls of desired size. Powder sugar your fingers while shaping candy. Place on cookie sheet and cool in refrigerator. In the top of double boiler over hot water, melt the baking chocolate, chocolate chips, butter and paraffin. Use a toothpick inserted in candy ball, dip in chocolate, place on waxed paper to harden. Variations: Coconut and red cherries may be added to candy instead of or with nuts. Any kind of flavoring may be used instead of vanilla.

Mrs. Wm. Onken
Hadley, Minnesota

TRUFFLES

12 ounces chocolate chips
1 15-ounce can Eagle brand
  sweetened condensed milk
Pinch salt
1 teaspoon vanilla or peppermint
  flavoring
6 tablespoons nuts, chopped

Dipping chocolate:
12 ounces chocolate chips
4 squares semi-sweet chocolate
2/3 of a bar (5x3-in.) of paraffin wax

Melt chocolate in double boiler. Remove from heat, add remaining ingredients and stir until smooth. Pour into buttered 9 x 9-in. pan and refrigerate. Cut into squares. Melt dipping chocolate ingredients together. Cool slightly before dipping squares. Place on waxed paper to harden.

Mrs. Emery Broschat
Cathay, North Dakota

OLD-FASHIONED CARAMELS

4 cups sugar
1/2 pound butter
1-1/2 cup dark Karo syrup
2 large cans evaporated milk
1 tablespoon vanilla

Bring sugar, butter and syrup to a hard boil in large, heavy saucepan. Punch small holes in cans of milk and slowly pour into boiling mixture. Keep the
(Continued on page 68)

CREAMY PARTY MINTS

2 tablespoons butter
2 tablespoons shortening
3 tablespoons warm water
5 cups confectioners sugar
Food coloring
Oil of flavorings

Combine butter, shortening, 2 tablespoons warm water and 2 cups confectioners sugar. Mix thoroughly. Add remaining sugar and 1 tablespoon water. Mix or knead until candy is smooth. Roll out to 1/8-in. thickness on waxed paper dusted with confectioners sugar. Cut into desired shapes. Or, press candy dough into sugared molds if you have them. Recipe may be divided into portions and colored with various colors and flavoring added. Suggestions: Blue with oil of spearmint; red with oil of cinnamon; yellow with oil of lemon; green with oil of wintergreen. Decorate top of mint with rosette made of icing.

Carol Crum
Marion, Ohio

FANNY FARMER CANDY

1/2 cup butter
3 cups powdered sugar
4 tablespoons whipping cream

syrup boiling all the while you are pouring in the milk. If boiling stops, discontinue pouring milk until mixture boils, then begin again to pour in the milk. Stir constantly until candy reaches the firm-ball stage, 244° on the candy thermometer. Remove from heat; add vanilla. Pour onto a buttered cookie sheet. A walnut half may be put on each piece of marked candy, or chopped nuts may be stirred in when adding vanilla. When cool, cut and wrap candy in individual squares.

Mrs. Ralph Niksch
Wanatah, Indiana

CRACKED GLASS HARD CANDY

    2 cups sugar (very fine granulated)
3/4 cup white syrup
    1 cup boiling water
1/4 teaspoon salt
    1 tablespoon butter
Red and green food coloring
Oils for flavoring: clove, cinnamon, peppermint, anise

Boil the cup of water in a large, heavy saucepan. Remove from heat and stir in the sugar, syrup, salt and butter. Return to heat, bring back to a boil and cover pan for about 3 minutes to allow steam to wash down any crystals on the sides of pan. Uncover and cook at high heat without stirring to hard-crack stage, 300°. Remove from heat and cool to 160° before adding color and flavoring. 1/4 teaspoon of clove, cinnamon or peppermint and 1/8 teaspoon anise is the suggested amount. Pour on a buttered cookie sheet and when cool enough to handle, cut into squares with scissors. Sprinkle with powdered sugar to prevent squares from sticking together.

Mrs. Virgil Davis
Edwardsville Illinois

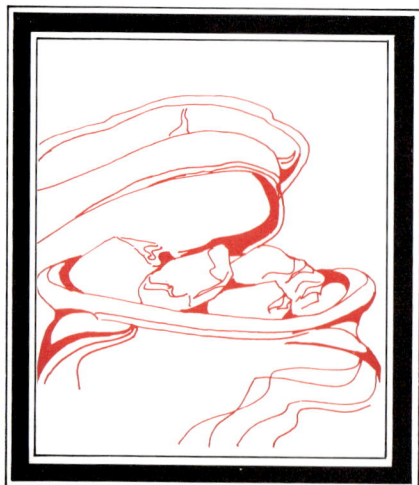

NEVER FAIL DIVINITY

    3 cups sugar
3/4 cup light corn syrup
3/4 cup water
    2 egg whites
    3-ounce box strawberry, raspberry OR lime gelatin
1/2 cup flaked coconut
    1 cup pecans OR walnuts, chopped

Combine sugar, corn syrup and water in heavy saucepan. Bring to boil. Cover pan and cook about 3 minutes until the steam has washed down any crystals that may have formed on the sides of the pan. Remove lid and cook over moderate heat, without stirring, to hard-ball stage, about 250°. While syrup is cooking, beat egg whites in large bowl until they just hold their shape, add gelatin and beat until stiff, but not dry. When syrup is ready, pour it slowly over egg whites in a steady thin stream whipping slowly at the same time. Toward the end, add the syrup more quickly and whip faster. Do not scrape pan. Beat constantly until candy holds shape. Fold in coconut and nuts. Pour into buttered 9 x 9-in. pan, cut into squares when cool. Or you may drop divinity onto a buttered surface by teaspoonfuls.

Beulah M. Hancock
Sumner, Washington

FRUIT FUDGE

    3 cups sugar
3/4 cup cream
3/4 cup milk
1/4 cup butter
    1 teaspoon almond extract
    1 cup coconut
1/4 cup candied cherries, chopped
1/4 cup candied pineapple, chopped

Combine sugar, cream, milk and butter in heavy saucepan. Boil until it reaches 236° or soft-ball stage. Remove from heat and allow to cool to lukewarm without stirring. Add flavoring, coconut, cherries and pineapple. Beat until creamy. Pour into buttered 10 x 6-in. pan. Cool. Cut in squares.

Mrs. Morris Jennings
Olney, Illinois

BUTTERMILK FUDGE

    3 cups sugar
1-1/2 cups buttermilk
1/4 pound butter

1-1/2 teaspoon soda
    1 teaspoon vanilla
    1 cup nuts, chopped

Place sugar, buttermilk, butter and soda in heavy 4-quart saucepan. Bring to boil over medium heat, stirring often as this mixture burns easily. Cook to 236° or soft-ball stage. Remove from heat and cool over cold water to lukewarm, do not stir. Stir in vanilla and nuts, beat until candy loses its gloss and thickens. Pour into buttered pan, cut into squares, cool completely.

Mrs. Leo L. Miller
Anchor, Illinois

VELVET FUDGE

1/4 cup butter
1/4 cup dark corn syrup or honey
    2 squares baking chocolate
1/2 cup whole milk
    2 cups sugar
Pinch salt
    1 teaspoon vanilla
    1 cup nuts, chopped

Melt butter, syrup and chocolate in heavy kettle over low heat. Stir often. Remove from heat and add milk, sugar and salt. Stir well, cook over medium heat to soft-ball stage, 238° on candy thermometer. Add vanilla and nuts. Do not beat. Let candy cool to lukewarm, then beat until fudge starts to lose its gloss and thickens. Pour into buttered 9 x 9-in. pan. Let harden, cut into squares.

Mrs. Alpha Sturlaugson
Dackoo, North Dakota

OKLAHOMA BROWN CANDY

    6 cups sugar
    1 stick butter
    2 cups light cream
1/4 teaspoon soda
    1 teaspoon vanilla
    2 pounds pecans, broken

Combine 4 cups sugar and cream in heavy 4-quart saucepan. Set aside. Put remaining 2 cups sugar in electric skillet on medium heat, stirring constantly until it starts to melt. Place sugar-cream mixture over low heat, stirring occasionally until sugar dissolves. Meanwhile continue to watch and stir sugar in electric skillet until it becomes light brown in color. Do not let it scorch! It will take about 30 minutes to brown.

Now *slowly* pour hot sugar in a *thin* stream into the sugar-cream mixture in saucepan, stirring constantly as you do this. Cook the combined mixture to the firm-ball stage, 246° on candy thermometer. Remove from heat and immediately stir in soda—this will foam up. Add butter, let stand 30 minutes to cool. Add vanilla and beat with wooden spoon until mixture loses its gloss and starts to thicken. Add pecans. Pour into buttered 9 x 13-in. pan. Cool, then cut into squares.

Frances Myers
Apache, Oklahoma

WHEATIES CANDY

1 pound Hersheys milk chocolate
Pinch salt
3 squares Bakers unsweetened
  chocolate
1 teaspoon butter
1 cup walnuts, coarsely chopped
5 cups Wheaties

Melt milk chocolate, salt, unsweetened chocolate and butter in top of double boiler over boiling water. Remove from heat, add walnuts and Wheaties and stir just enough to coat cereal. Drop by teaspoonfuls onto waxed paper. Let harden at room temperature.

Mrs. Penn Peek
Bluffton, Indiana

CANDY-COATED NUTS

  1 cup brown sugar
1/2 cup granulated sugar
1/2 cup dairy sour cream
  1 teaspoon vanilla
  2 cups walnut halves

Combine sugars and sour cream in saucepan. Cook over medium heat, stirring until sugar is dissolved. Continue cooking, without stirring, until candy thermometer reaches 236° or soft-ball stage. Remove from heat. Add vanilla and walnuts. Stir gently until nuts are well coated. Spread on waxed paper and separate walnuts

with a fork. Let dry. These candied nuts freeze very well.

Marsha Nelson
Chanute, Kansas

FRUIT CANDY

1/2 pound marshmallows
  1 small package figs
1/2 pound dates
1/2 pound blanched almonds, chopped
1/2 pound pecans or walnuts, chopped
  1 cup shredded coconut
  1 small jar maraschino cherries,
    drained, chopped

Grind figs and dates. Melt marshmallows, add fruit, nuts, coconut and cherries, mix well. Pour into buttered pan. Cool. Cut into squares, roll in granulated sugar.

Mrs. Earl Carlson
Chokio, Minnesota

APPLE BALLS

    2 eggs, beaten
    2 cups confectioners sugar
    1 cup dates OR raisins, chopped
    1 cup dried apples, chopped
    2 cups shredded coconut
    2 cups nuts, chopped
1-1/2 cup peanut butter
    3 cups chocolate chips
  1/3 bar paraffin

Combine and mix thoroughly all ingredients, except chocolate chips and paraffin. Shape into balls of desired size. Chill. Melt chocolate chips and paraffin in small pan. Insert toothpick into apple balls, dip in chocolate to coat. Place on waxed paper to harden. Store in tightly covered container.

Mrs. Carl A. Koenig
Loganville, Wisconsin

CHERRY PEANUT SLICES

    2 cups marshmallows
    2 teaspoons water
  1/3 cup candied cherries, chopped
  1/2 teaspoon vanilla
    2 cups confectioners sugar
   24 caramel candies
1-1/2 tablespoons light cream
    1 cup salted peanuts, chopped

Melt marshmallows and water in top of double boiler over boiling water. Remove from heat, stir in cherries,

vanilla and confectioners sugar. Mixture will be firm. Turn onto a board dusted with 1 tablespoon of confectioners sugar and knead 2 to 3 minutes until smooth. Form into 3 rolls 3/4 x 6 in. long. Set aside at room temperature about 30 minutes. Melt caramels and cream in top of double boiler. Remove from heat. Spread peanuts on large piece of waxed paper. Spread caramel mixture over marshmallow roll, then quickly roll in peanuts. Repeat with remaining 2 candy rolls. Wrap in waxed paper, set aside for 1 hour at room temperature. Slice to serve.

Mrs. Galen Eikenberry
Scottville, Michigan

PULLED MINTS

3 cups sugar
6 scant tablespoons butter
1 cup cold water
Food coloring
Oil of peppermint, spearmint
  or wintergreen

Combine sugar, butter and water in heavy 2-1/2-quart saucepan. Stir just enough to moisten sugar. Boil until mixture reaches 260°. Pour immediately onto cold, lightly buttered marble slab or heavy stoneware platter. Do not scrape pan! Keep turning candy mixture onto cooler spot on marble slab or platter. Pull a few minutes. Drop 6 to 8 drops of flavoring, then 6 or 7 drops of food coloring into mixture. Pull until like taffy using a small amount of butter on your hands. Shape into twisted ropes, cut into pieces with kitchen shears. Place on cookie sheets, don't let pieces touch. Keep in cold place overnight. Store in airtight tins 2 to 3 days to "season" and become minty. Do not make this candy on a rainy day!

Donna J. Miller
Groveport, Ohio

CHOCOLATE DRIZZLED PECAN PENUCHE

    2 cups granulated sugar
    2 cups light brown sugar
    1/2 cup light cream
    1/2 cup milk
    2 tablespoons butter
    1 cup pecans, coarsely chopped
1-1/2 teaspoon vanilla
    1/2 cup chocolate chips
    24 pecan halves

Butter sides only of heavy 2-1/2-quart saucepan. Add sugars, cream, milk and butter. Place over medium heat, stirring just until sugars dissolve and mixture boils. Boil without stirring until candy thermometer reaches 238° or soft-ball stage. Immediately remove from heat, cool to 110° without stirring. Add pecans and vanilla. Now you may use your electric mixer. Beat candy at high speed until it becomes thick and begins to lose its gloss—watch carefully. Quickly pour into buttered 8 x 8-in. pan spreading evenly. While still warm, but firm, cut into 24 pieces with sharp knife. Cool. When cool, melt chocolate chips. Using a teaspoon, drizzle chocolate over top of candy. Top each piece of candy with a pecan half. Store in tightly covered container.

Mrs. Bill Umbarger
Fairfax, Missouri

ROYAL BRITTLE

    1 cup walnut halves
    1 cup pecan halves
    1 cup almonds
    1 cup filberts
    1/2 cup pistachio nuts, halved
    3/4 cup EACH red and green
        candied cherries, halved
1-1/2 cup candied pineapple, chopped
    2 cups sugar
    1 cup water
    3/4 cup light corn syrup
    1/2 teaspoon orange extract

Combine nuts and fruit; mix well. Spread 1/2 in. thick on 15 x 10 x 1-in. buttered jelly roll pan. Cook remaining ingredients to 300° or hard-ball stage. Pour hot syrup over fruit. When firm, cut with sharp knife into 5 dozen, 1-1/2-in. pieces. Store in covered container.

Alberta Hanson
Cushing, Wisconsin

APLETS

    4 envelopes unflavored gelatin
2-1/2 cups applesauce
3-1/3 cups sugar
    1/8 teaspoon salt
    1 cup nuts, chopped
    2 teaspoons vanilla
    1/2 teaspoon rose extract
    1/4 teaspoon lemon extract

Soak gelatin in 1 cup applesauce for 10 minutes. Bring to boil remainder of applesauce, sugar and salt. Add gelatin applesauce mixture. Boil hard for 15 minutes. Cool slightly. Add nuts, vanilla and extracts. Pour into well buttered 9 x 13-in. pan. Set to dry overnight. Cut into squares, roll in confectioners sugar. Dry several hours more.

Mrs. Allen Sayler
Hebron, North Dakota

EDITOR'S NOTE: The following recipes and instructions for dipping candy in chocolate are from Dorothy Chambers of Mansfield, Ohio.

Dorothy and her husband, James, have a grain and livestock operation— and produce maple syrup. You'll note two of her recipes, Maple Caramel Marshmallows and Maple Fudge, include maple syrup as an ingredient. She sent us samples of these candies made from fresh-from-the-farm syrup—yummy!

HOW TO DIP CANDY IN CHOCOLATE: To melt chocolate for dipping, grate dipping chocolate or cut in small pieces. Bring water to boiling point in bottom of double boiler. *REMOVE FROM HEAT.* Place chocolate in top of double boiler over hot water and stir often until melted. Remove from hot water and fill bottom of double boiler with lukewarm water and place chocolate over warm water. It is very important not to let chocolate get warmer than lukewarm. Also, be very careful not to get any water or steam in chocolate. One drop of water can ruin a whole batch of chocolate. Dip chocolates with dipping fork or use fingers. You can make your own dipping fork from a piece of wire about 8-in. long. Bend the one end into a small circle about 1-in. in diameter and then bend wire at circle as to form an "L" shape.

MAPLE CARAMEL MARSHMALLOWS

Marshmallow:
    2 cups granulated sugar, sifted
    3/4 cup hot water
    1/2 cup light corn syrup
    1/2 cup maple syrup
1-1/2 teaspoons maple flavoring
2-1/2 tablespoons unflavored gelatin
    3/4 cup cold water

Combine the two syrups, then divide in 1/2 cups. Dissolve gelatin in cold water, stir well. Let stand at least 5 minutes. In a 1 or 2 quart saucepan, combine sugar, hot water and 1/2 cup of syrup. Blend well, cook over high heat to 240° during cold weather, 242° during warm weather. Do not stir after boiling begins. When mixture reaches desired temperature, shut off heat and at once add the remaining 1/2 cup of syrup and the gelatin. Stir gently for a few seconds. Pour at once into an 8-in. Pyrex bowl. Immediately start to beat, increasing speed to highest point after first minute or two. Beat for about 10 minutes or until the consistency of whipped cream. Add maple flavoring toward end of beating. Fold in 1/4 cup finely chopped pecans. Pour in lightly greased 9 x 13-in. pan.

Refrigerate at least 8 hours. Marshmallow may be prepared a day or two in advance. Note: You may use maple-flavored syrup or all light corn syrup in place of maple syrup. You may also use vanilla or any other flavoring in place of maple flavoring.

Caramel:
1-1/3 cup granulated sugar
1-1/3 cup light corn syrup
    3/4 cup whipping cream
    1/4 cup water
    3 tablespoons butter
    1/4 teaspoon salt
    1 teaspoon vanilla

Combine the whipping cream and water in a small saucepan and heat to just below the boiling point. In a 3-quart saucepan, combine the sugar, syrup and half of the cream. Bring to boiling point. Let cook about 5 minutes, adjusting heat to prevent boiling over. Then slowly add rest of warm cream, a little at a time.

Let cook about 5 more minutes, then add butter. Continue to cook rapidly, lowering heat toward end to prevent scorching. Stir occasionally and cook to 240° during cold weather, 242° during warm weather. Remove from heat, add salt and vanilla, stirring gently. Let cool to about 175º, stirring it very gently 2 or 3 times as it cools.

To assemble candy: Remove marshmallow from pan and place on cutting board. Carefully pour caramel over marshmallow, spreading it as uniformly as possible on top only. Use a greased knife for spreading. Let stand in cold place, or refrigerator, making test with large heavy greased knife until caramel is firm enough to cut. Place candy, caramel side down, on board when cutting it into squares. This is important to prevent crushing candy. Cut into squares. Rub knife with shortening often to prevent sticking. If caramel sticks to knife, place candy back in refrigerator to chill for a few minutes. Dip squares of candy in chocolate. Let cool with caramel side up.

MAPLE FUDGE

2 cups maple syrup
1 tablespoon light corn syrup
3/4 cup light cream
1 teaspoon vanilla
1/2 cup pecans, chopped

Combine syrups and cream in heavy 2-quart saucepan and cook over low heat. Stir constantly until mixture begins to boil; continue cooking without stirring until candy reaches 236º. Remove from heat; cool to lukewarm without stirring or beating. Beat with · electric mixer on low speed until candy loses its gloss and thickens. This takes quite awhile. Stir in vanilla and nuts. Pour into lightly buttered 8 x 4 x 2-in.

pan. While still warm, cut in pieces. Makes about 1 pound.

MELTAWAY MINTS

1 pound dipping milk chocolate
1-1/2 tablespoons shortening, melted to to about 130º
1/4 cup scalded whipping cream, cooled to 130º
1/4 teaspoon oil of peppermint or 1 tablespoon peppermint extract

Cut up and melt chocolate in upper part of double boiler. Heat water in bottom of double boiler to boiling. Remove from heat and place top of boiler with chocolate over hot water. Stir often until chocolate is melted. Do not let chocolate get too hot. Pour chocolate in warm 7 or 8-in. bowl. Add warm melted fat, a little at a time, beating until well blended. Add warm cream all at once, add peppermint; immediately beat at low speed until smooth for about 1 minute, then beat 1 minute more.

If preparation separates or curdles during the beating process, place back in double boiler over simmering water and beat until smooth. May be necessary to add a teaspoon or two of water (not more than 1 tablespoon). This condition is caused if ingredients are too cool, or when chocolate does not contain enough moisture. When smooth, pour into waxed-paper-lined 8 x 8-in. pan and spread evenly. Cover and refrigerate at least 3 days. Cut into squares. Dip in green chocolate if desired. Be sure mints are very cold when dipped.

PEANUT BUTTER CUPS

2 cups peanut butter
6 tablespoons butter
2 teaspoons salt
1 pound confectioners sugar

Mix all ingredients together well. Fill bonbon cups about 1/2 full of melted chocolate. Add small ball of the peanut butter mixture. Fill cup with chocolate. Let set until firm.

MICROWAVE OVEN CHOCOLATE FUDGE

1/2 pound marshmallows (4 cups miniature or 32 large)
1/4 cup butter
2/3 cup evaporated milk
1-1/2 cup sugar
1/4 teaspoon salt
12 ounces milk chocolate chips
1 teaspoon vanilla
1 cup nuts, chopped

Combine marshmallows, butter, milk, sugar and salt in 3-quart casserole. Cook until mixture boils, 8 minutes; stir. Cook 3 minutes longer. Remove from heat, add chocolate chips and beat until chocolate melts. Use electric mixer for smoother fudge. Add vanilla and nuts. Pour into buttered 9-in. square pan. Cool until firm, cut into squares. Makes 2-1/2 pounds. For a special treat, dip the squares of fudge in chocolate.

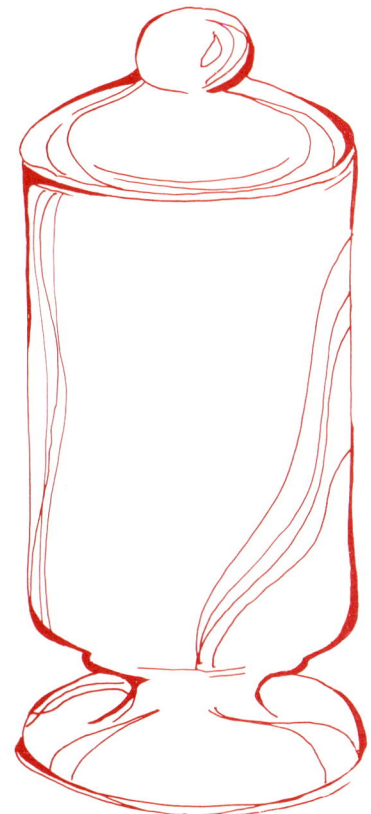

Patterns

SANTA BOW COUNTER

Directions on page 3

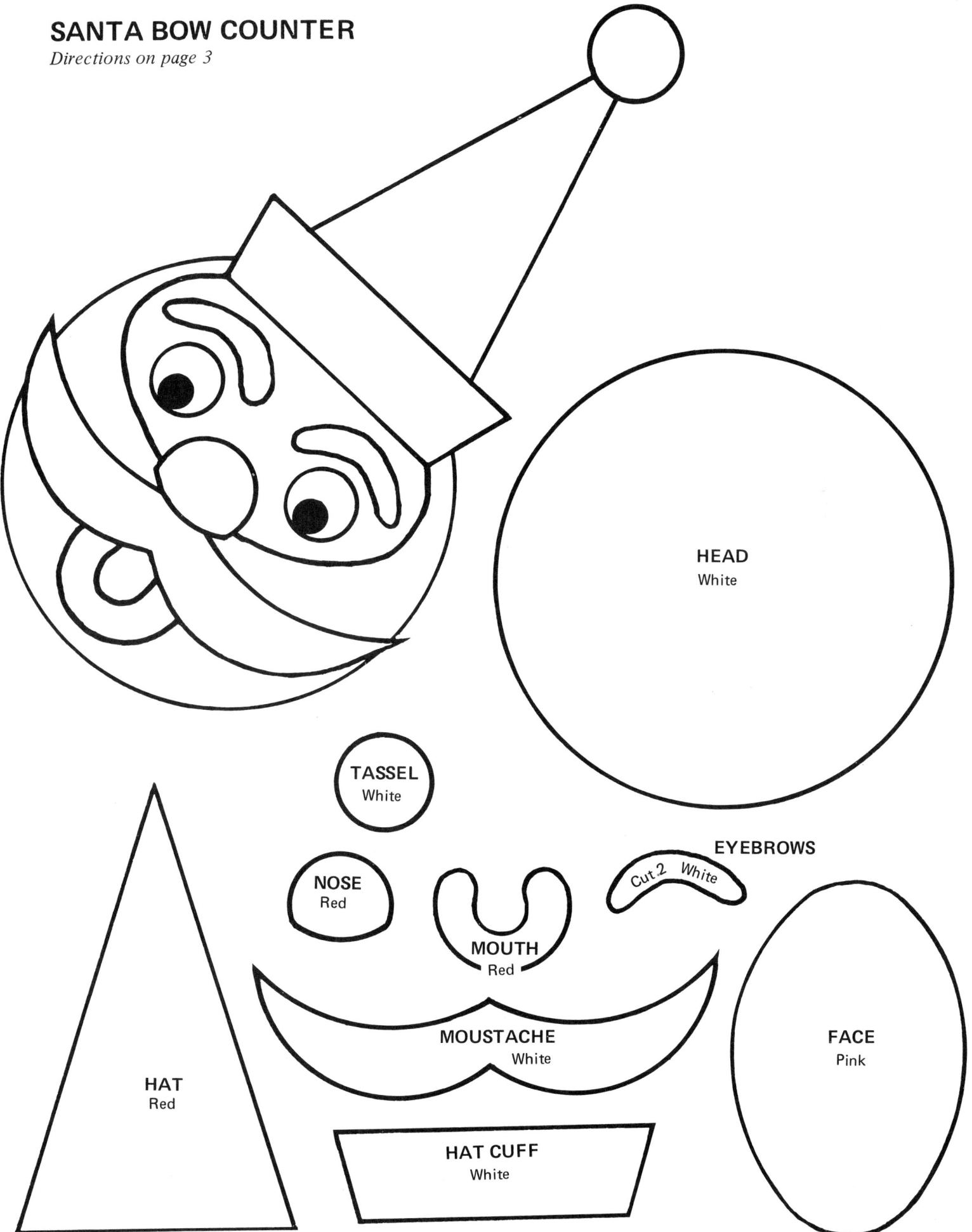

HEAD
White

TASSEL
White

EYEBROWS

Cut 2   White

NOSE
Red

MOUTH
Red

MOUSTACHE
White

FACE
Pink

HAT
Red

HAT CUFF
White

SLEIGH SCENE
Directions on page 10

Glue Flap

Fold

SLEIGH RUNNERS

Fold

Fold

Glue to Sleigh Bottom

SLEIGH BACK PANEL

Fold

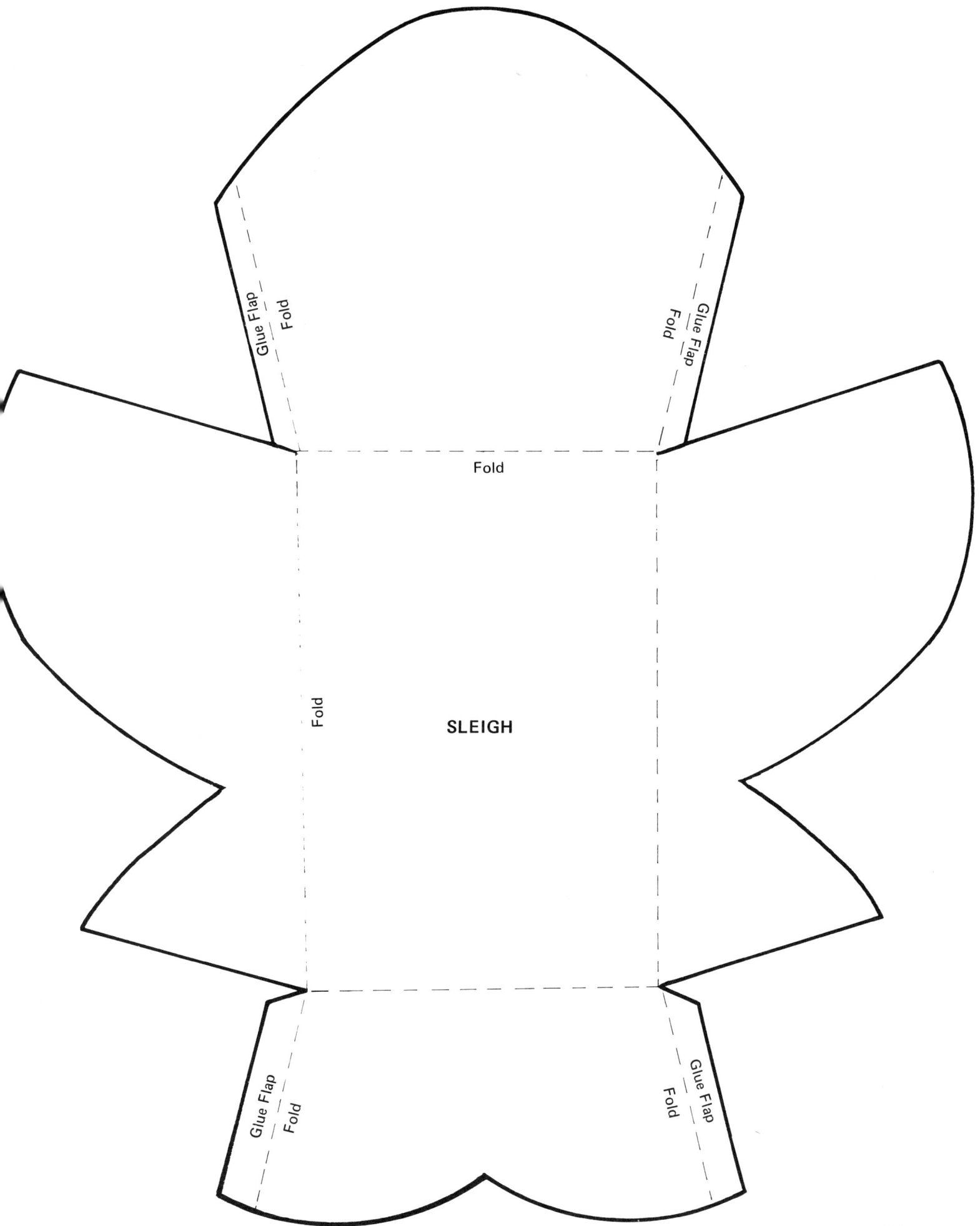

Glue Flap

Fold

Glue Flap

Fold

Fold

Fold

SLEIGH

Glue Flap

Fold

Glue Flap

Fold

77

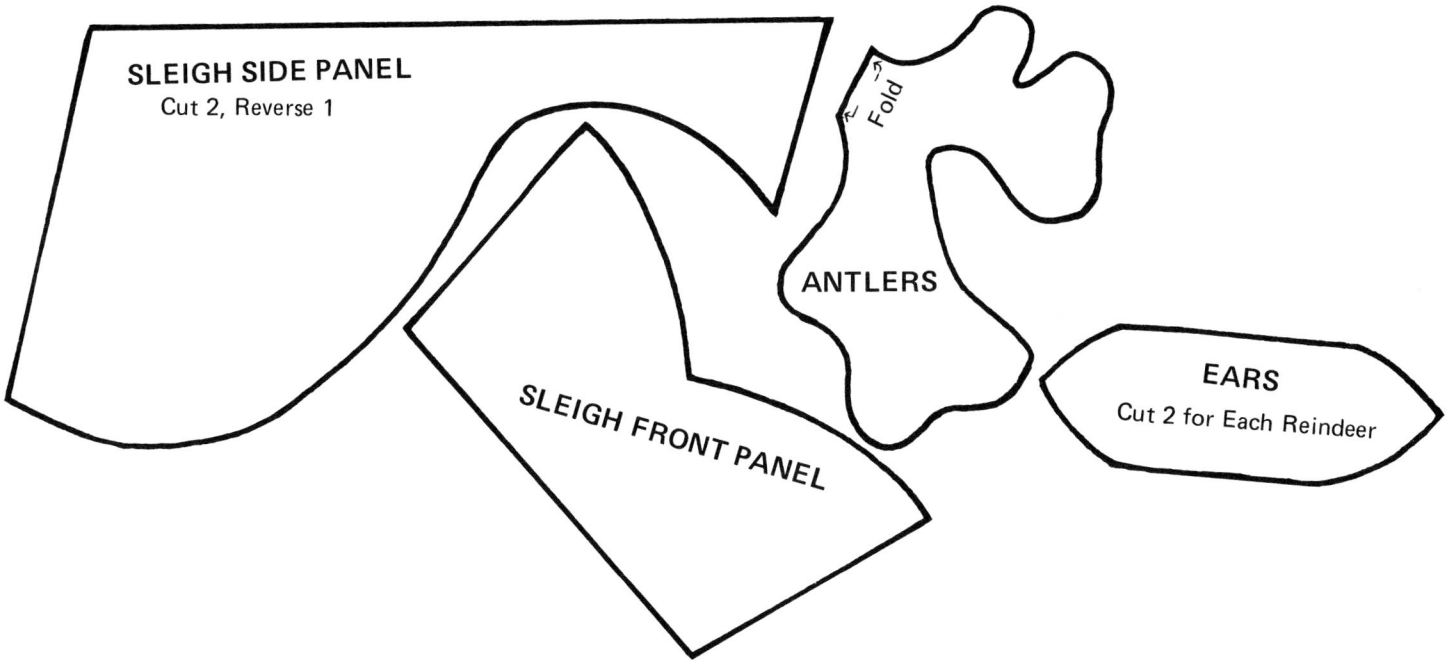

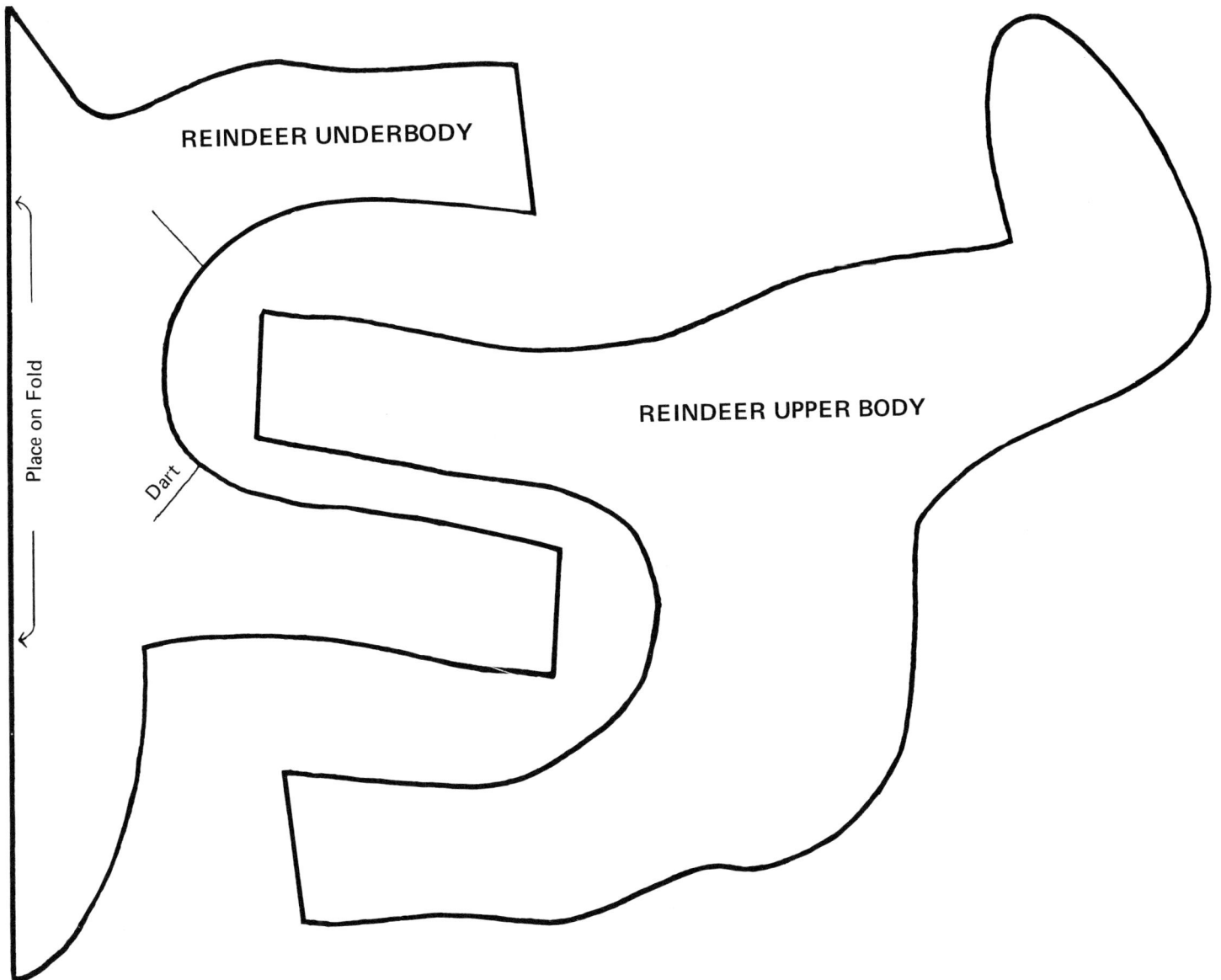

WINGS
Cut 1

BODY
Cut 1 of Cloth
Cut 1 of Cardboard

ARMS
Cut 1 of Cardboard
Cut 1 of Cloth

HURRICANE SANTA
Directions on page 19

MOUTH

Red

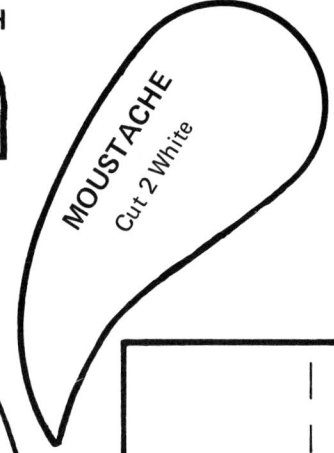

MOUSTACHE
Cut 2 White

BEARD
White

Seam Line

Stitch on This Line

HAT BAND
White

HAT
Red

EYEBROW
Cut 2 White

NOSE

Red

PUPIL

Cut 2 Black

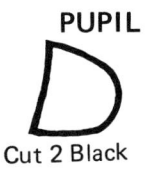

EYE
Cut 2 White

NEEDLEPOINT ORNAMENTS
Directions on pages 21-22

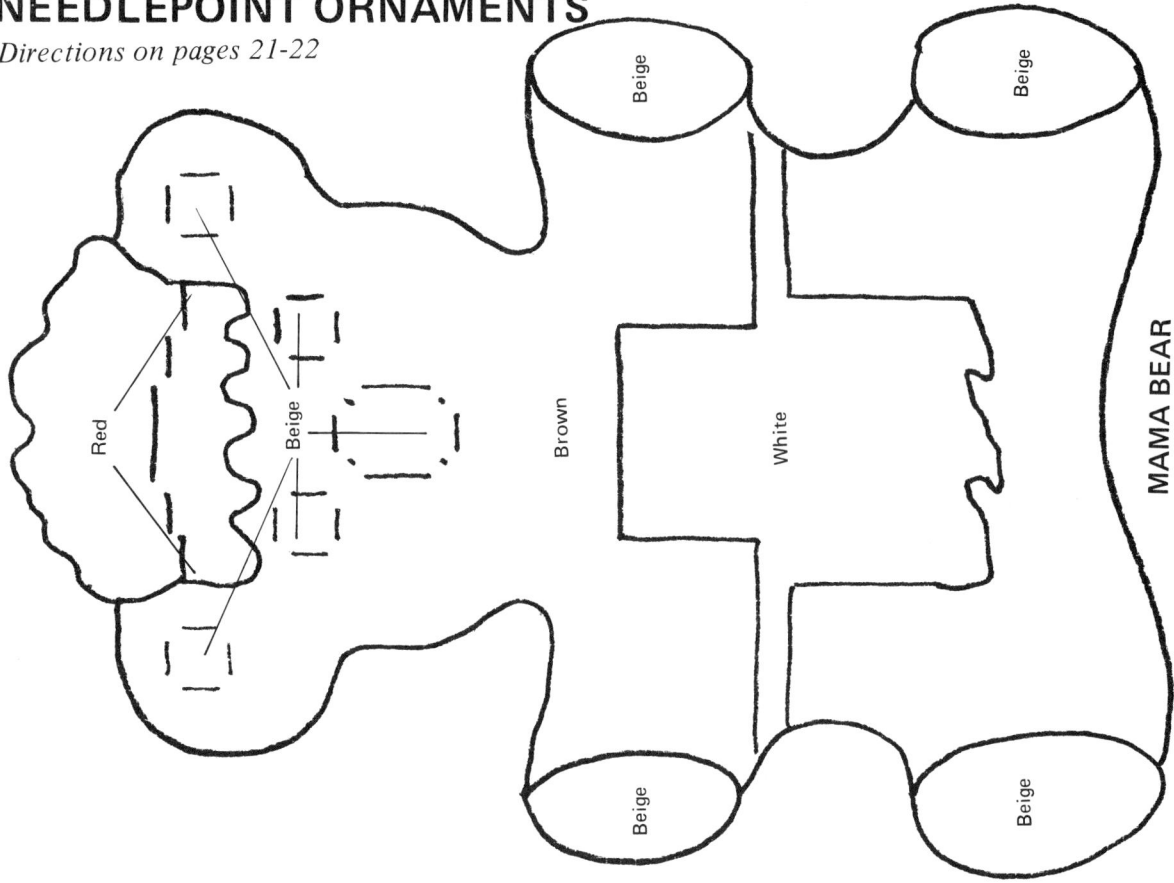

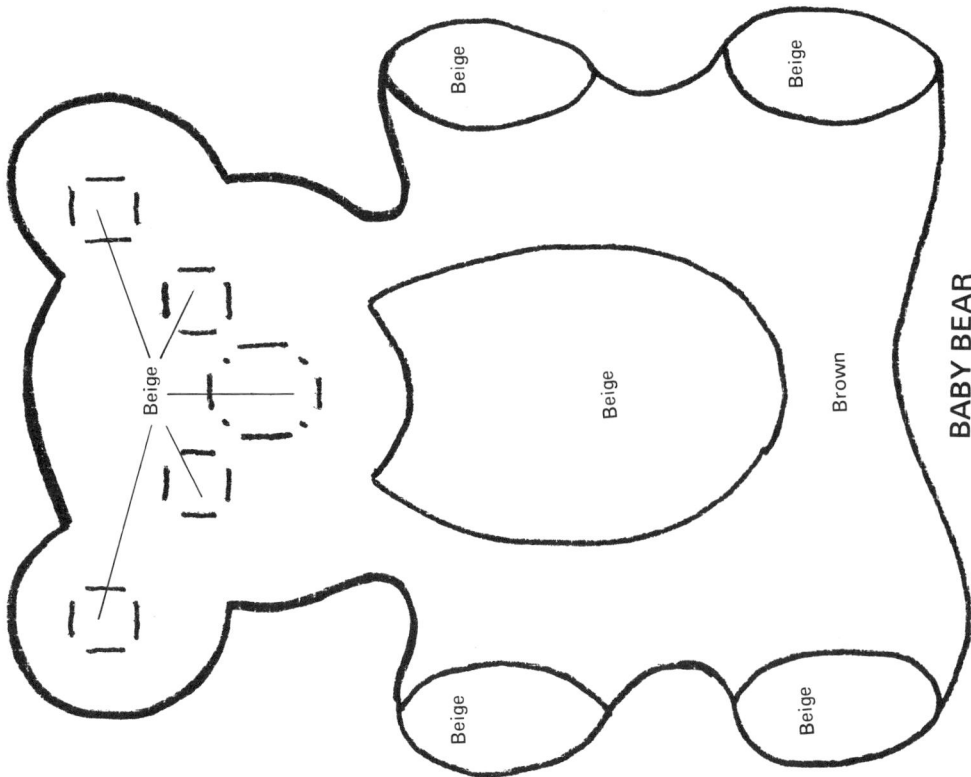

Beige

Beige

Red

Beige

Brown

White

Beige

Beige

MAMA BEAR

Beige

Beige

Beige

Beige

Brown

BABY BEAR

Beige

Beige

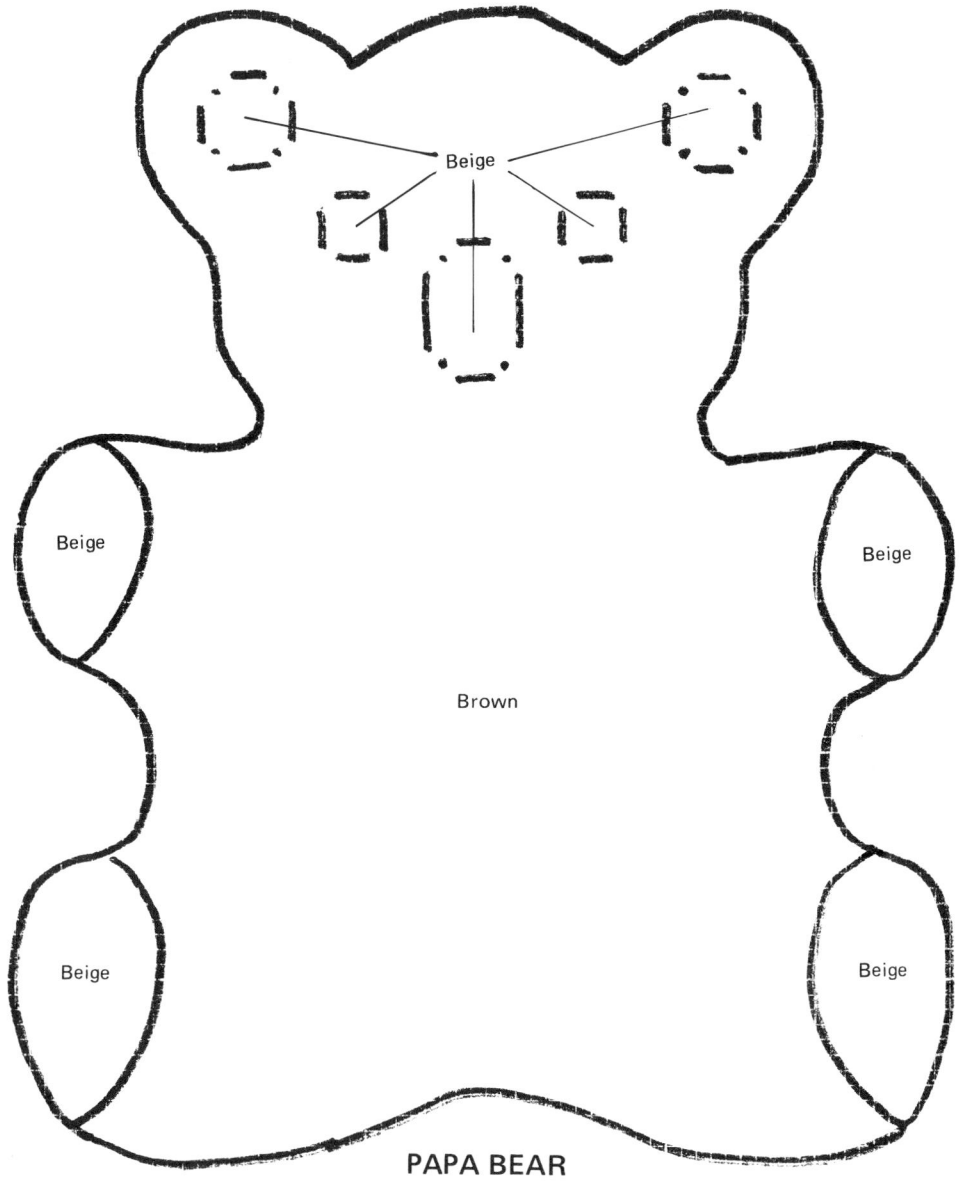

Beige

Beige

Beige

Brown

Beige

Beige

PAPA BEAR

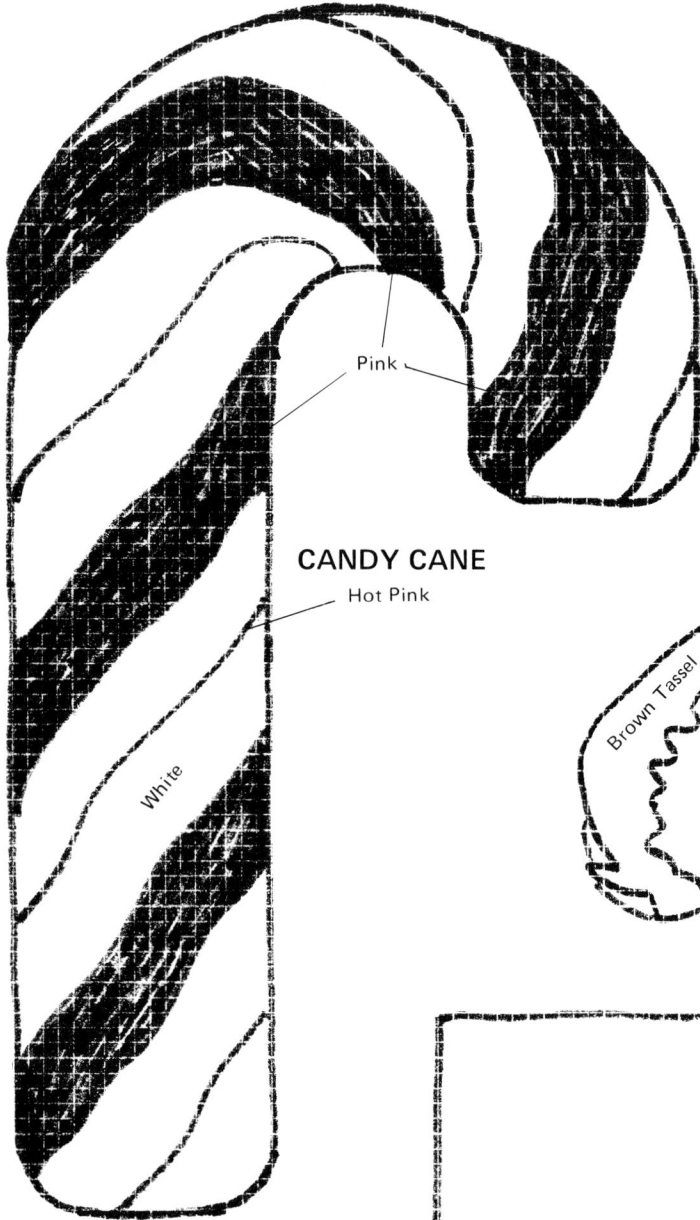

CANDY CANE

Pink

Hot Pink

White

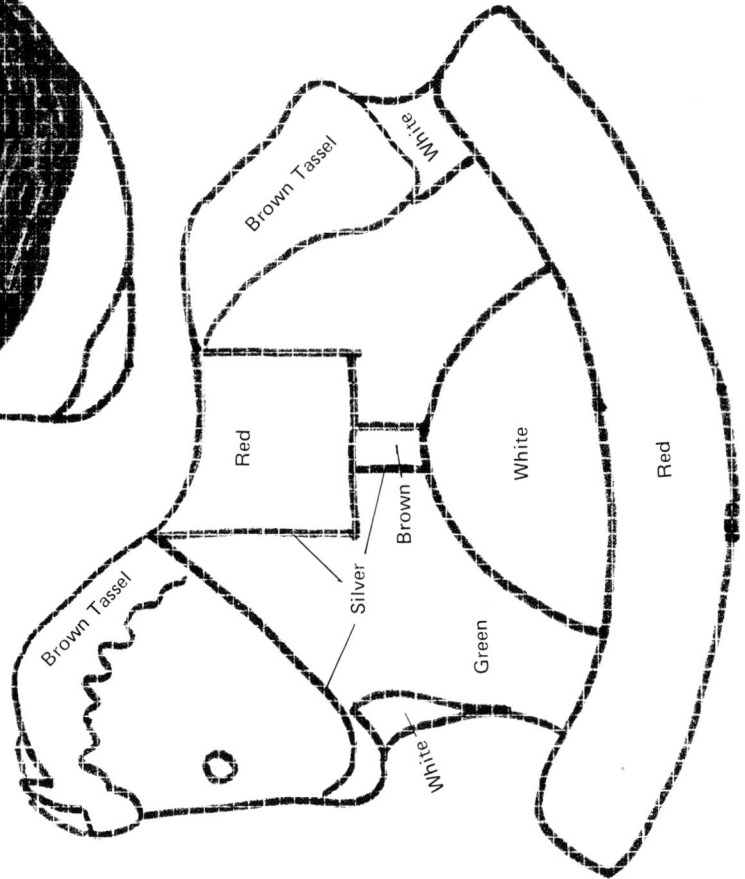

ROCKING HORSE

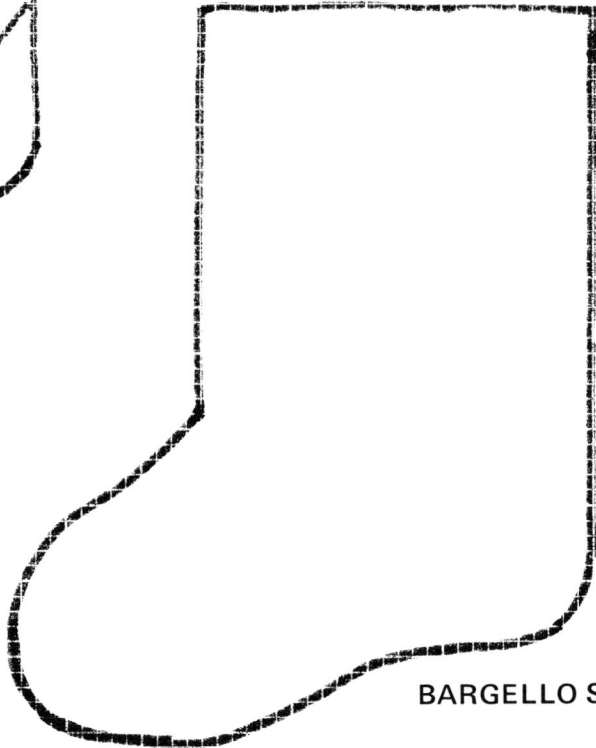

Brown Tassel

White

Brown Tassel

Red

Silver

Brown

White

Red

Green

White

Zigzag Pattern

Alternate Red and White

Green Stitch at Peaks of White Zigzag

BARGELLO STOCKING

red ∘ blue ˋ
dk. red ˊ pink ▪x
flesh · lt. red ▪
lt. gray -

SANTA HOUSE

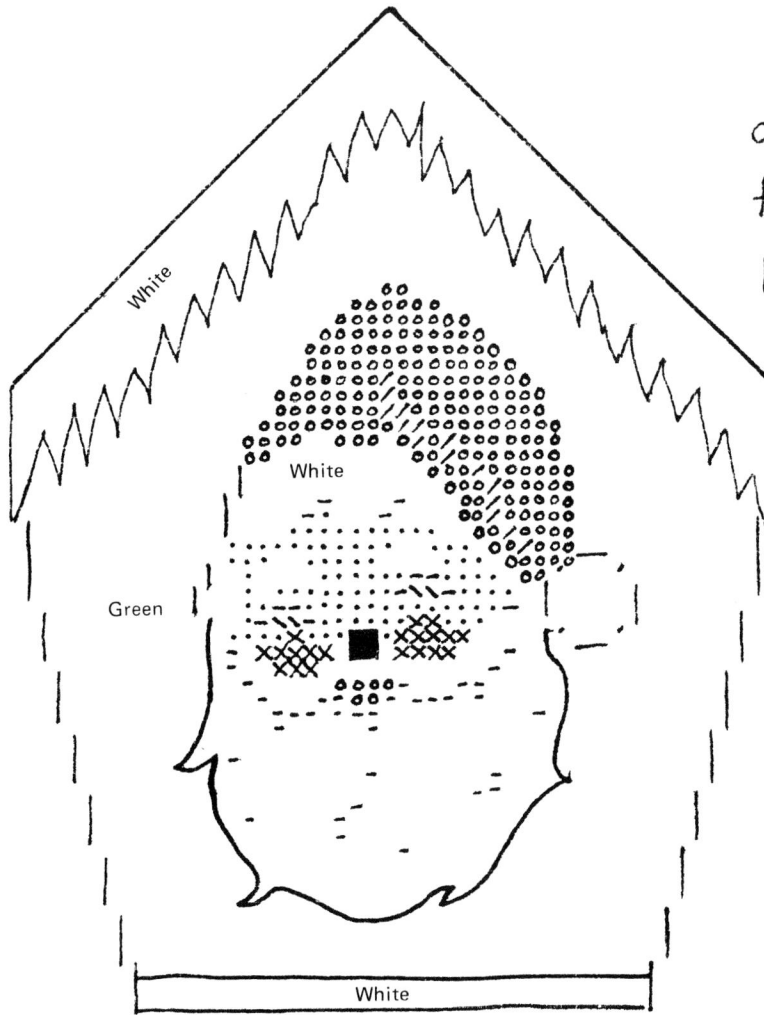

White

White

Green

White

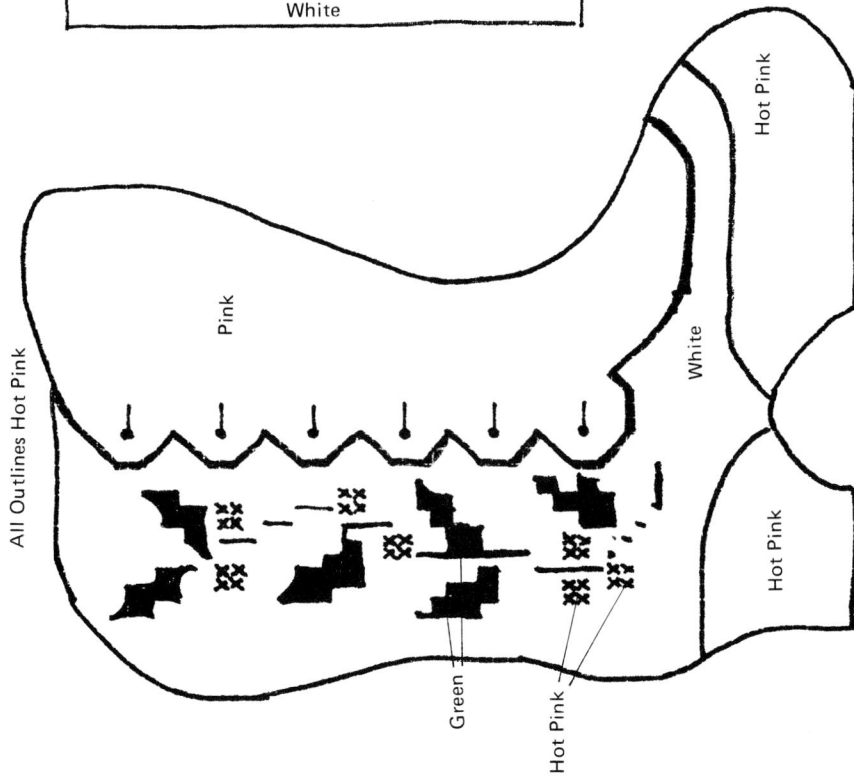

FRENCH BOOT

Hot Pink

Hot Pink

Pink

White

All Outlines Hot Pink

Hot Pink

Green

Hot Pink

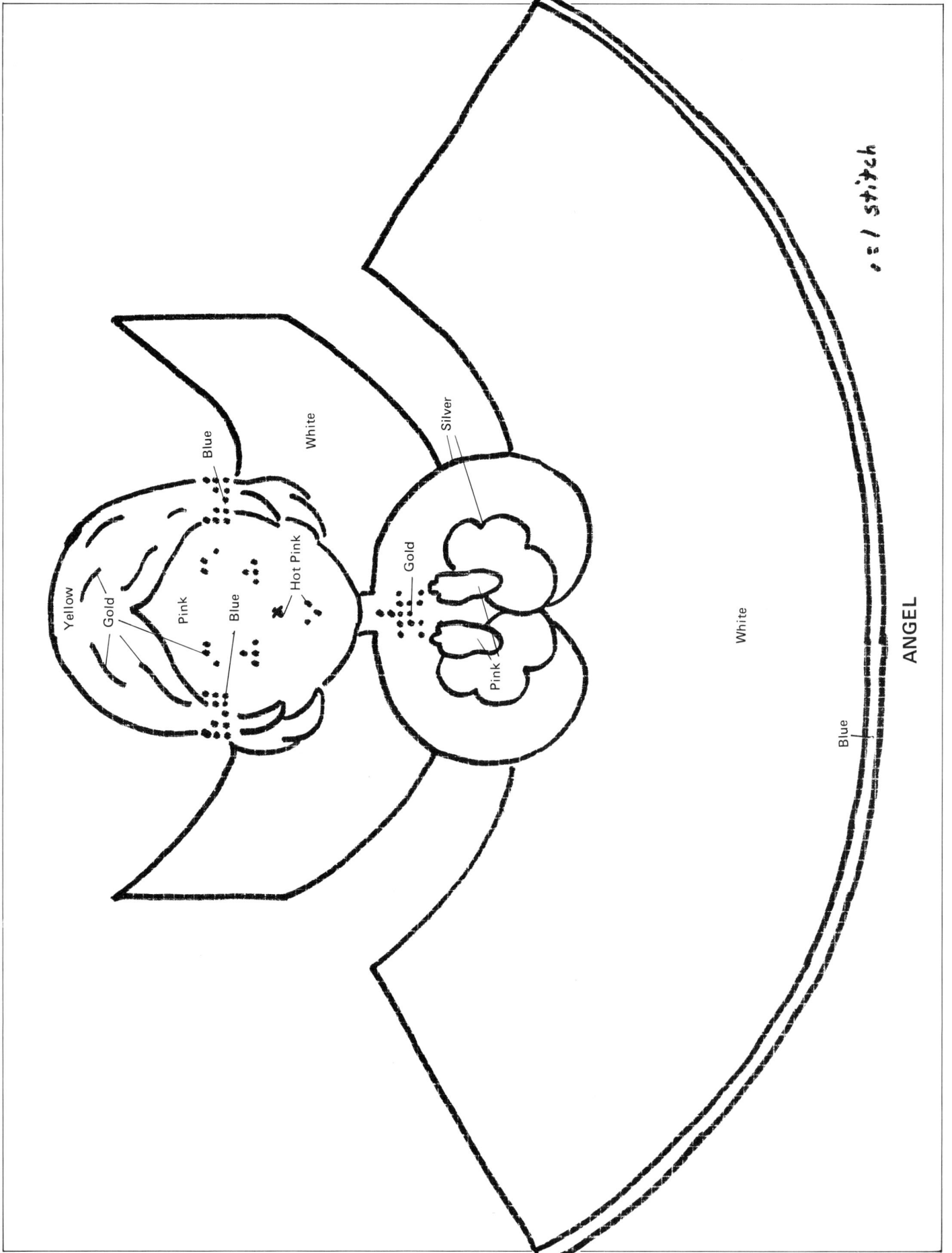

Blue

White

Silver

Yellow

Gold

Gold

Pink

Blue

Hot Pink

Gold

Pink

stitch 1:0'

White

Blue

ANGEL

88

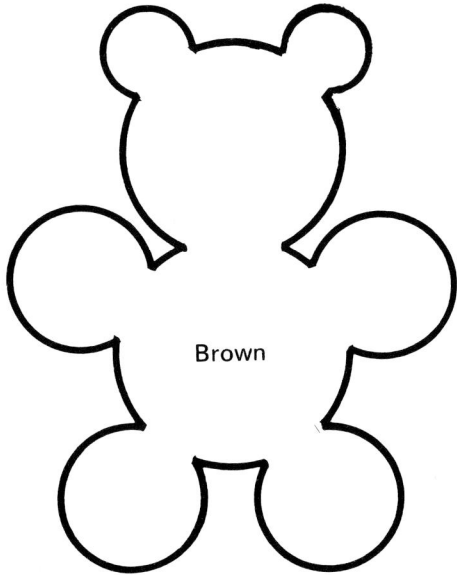

Brown

POM-POM AND FELT ORNAMENTS

Directions on page 25

TEDDY BEAR

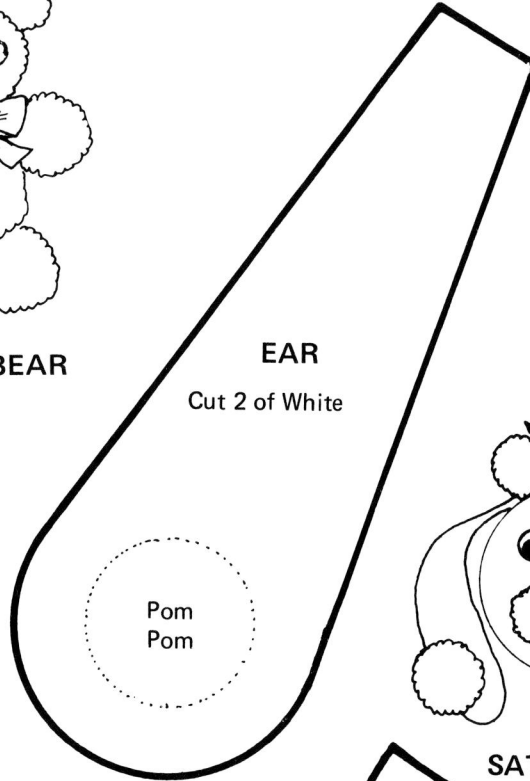

EAR

Cut 2 of White

Pom Pom

SATIN POODLE BALL

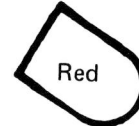

Red

TONGUE

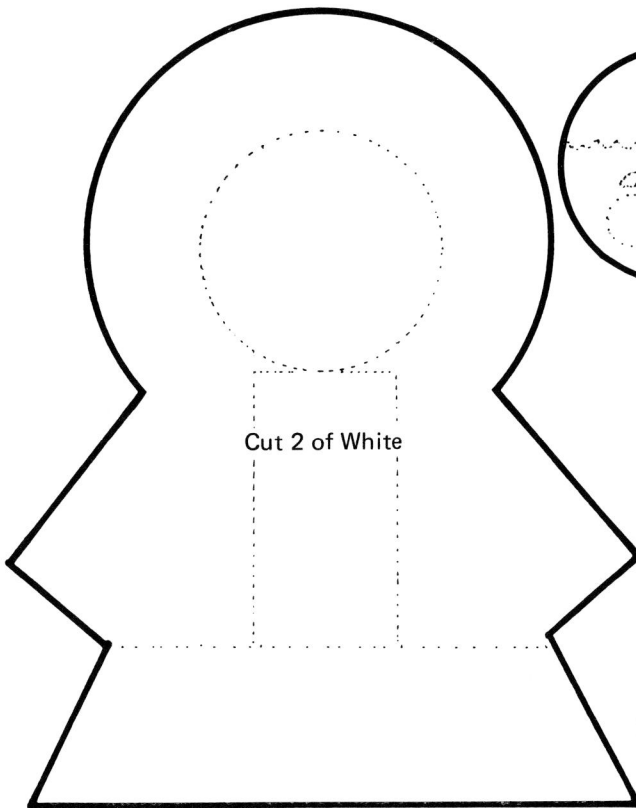

Cut 2 of White

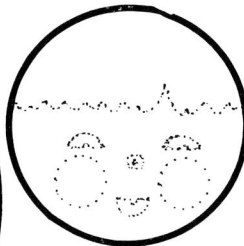

FACE

Pink

Cut 4 of Red

MITTEN

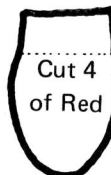

BOOTS

Cut 2 of Black

Sequin

ESKIMO

HAIR

Black

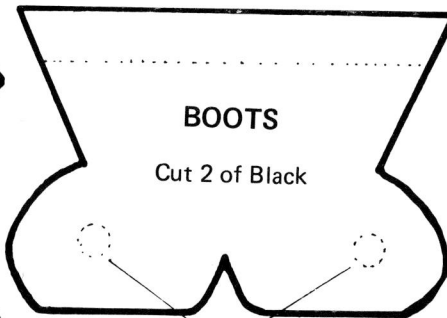

FISH

Cut 2 of Black

SANTA

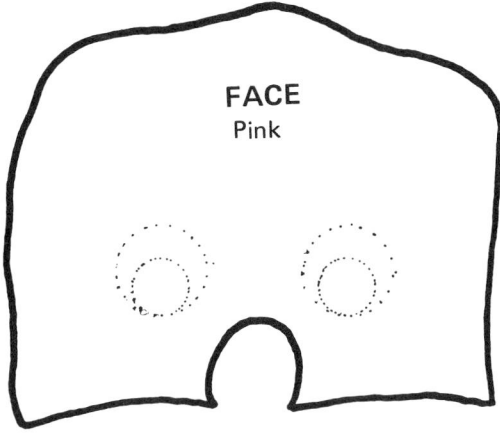

FACE
Pink

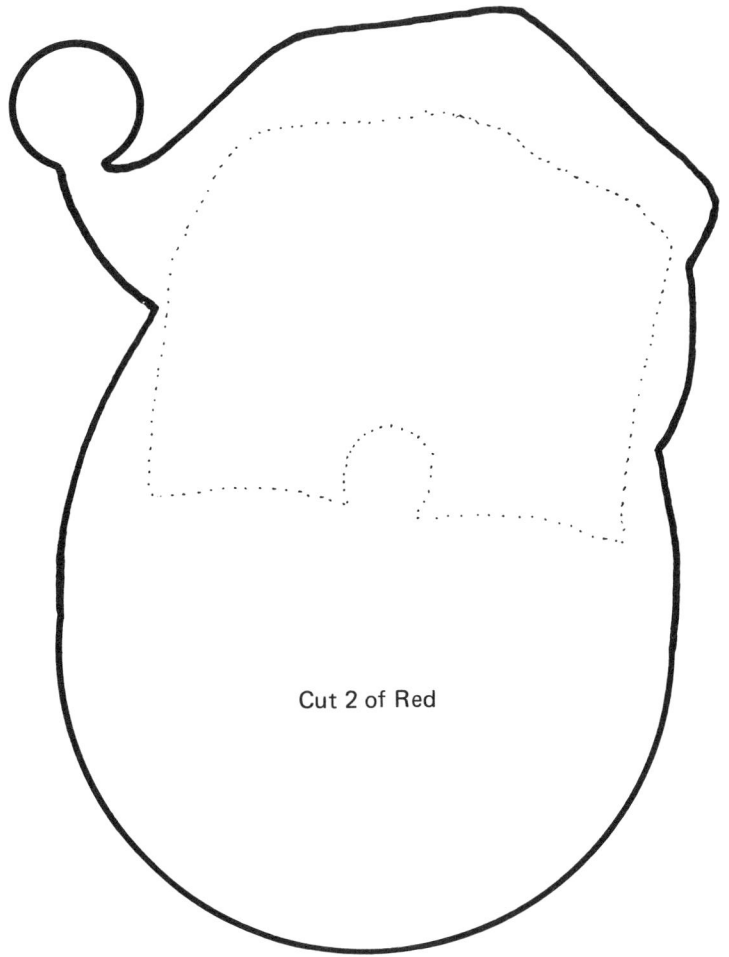

Cut 2 of Red

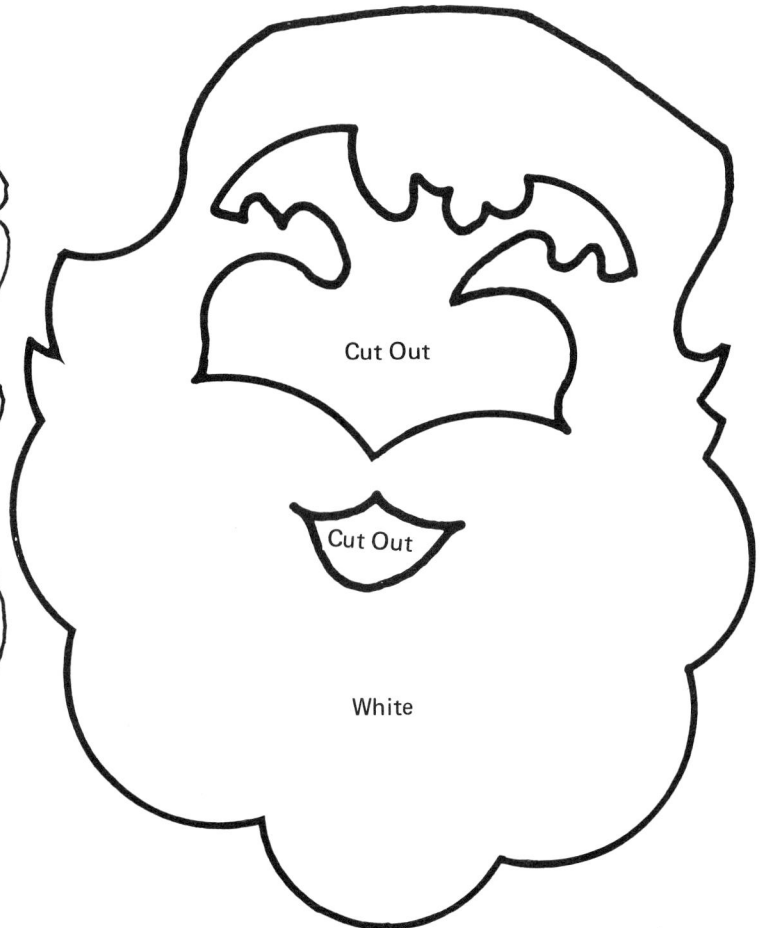

Cut Out

Cut Out

White

FOAM AND FELT ORNAMENTS
Directions on page 26

Cut Foam on This Line

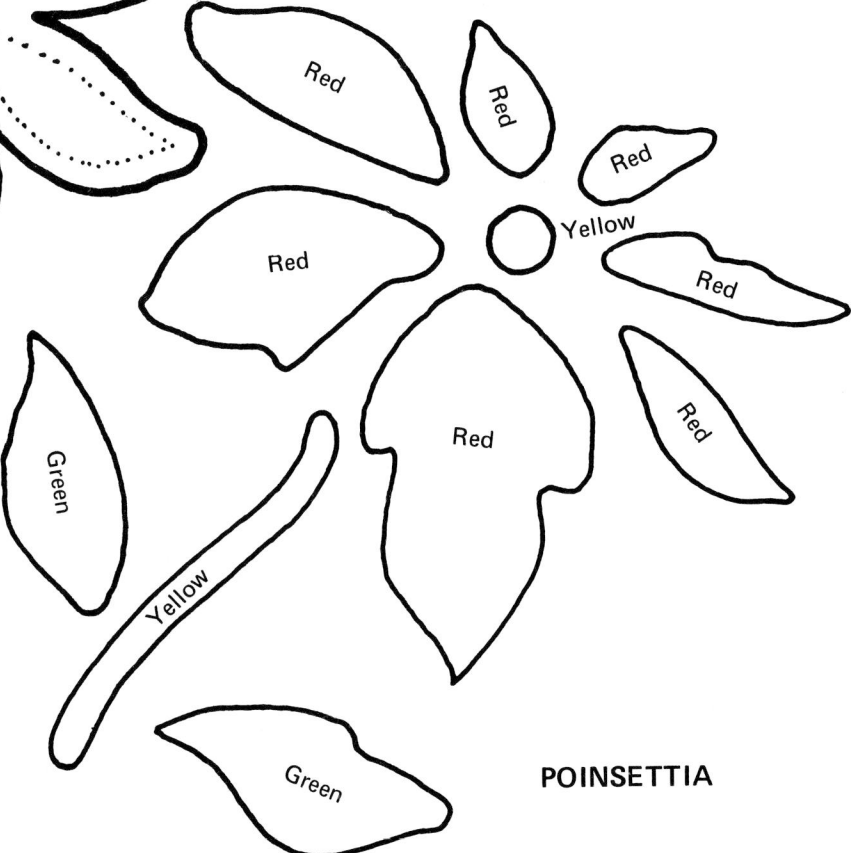

Red

Red

Red

Red

Red

Yellow

Red

Red

Green

Yellow

Red

Green

POINSETTIA

SNOWMAN

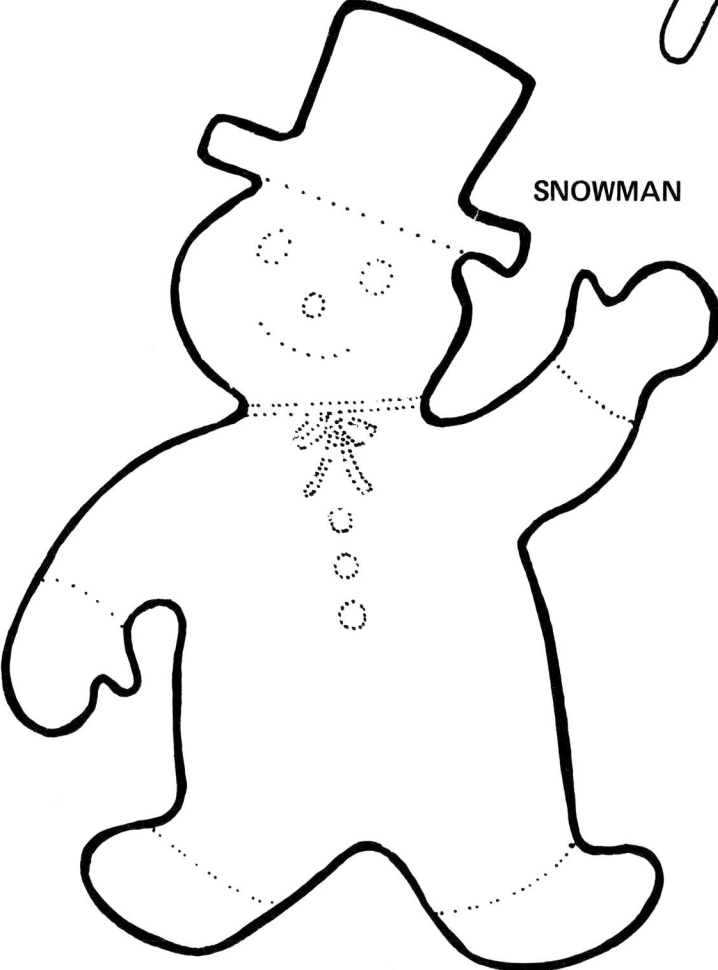

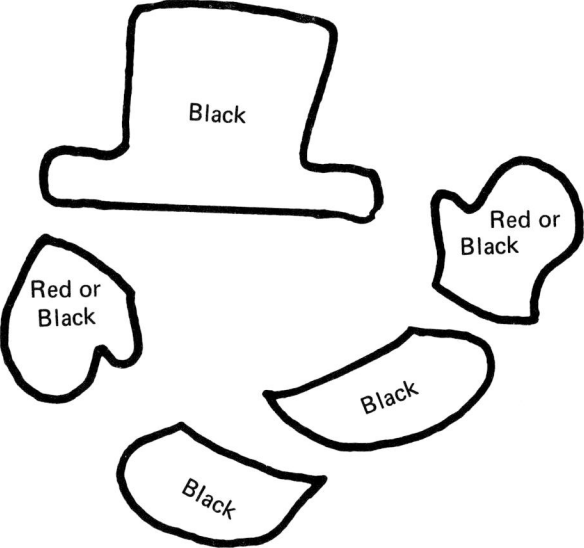

Black

Red or Black

Red or Black

Black

Black

CHRISTMAS TREE

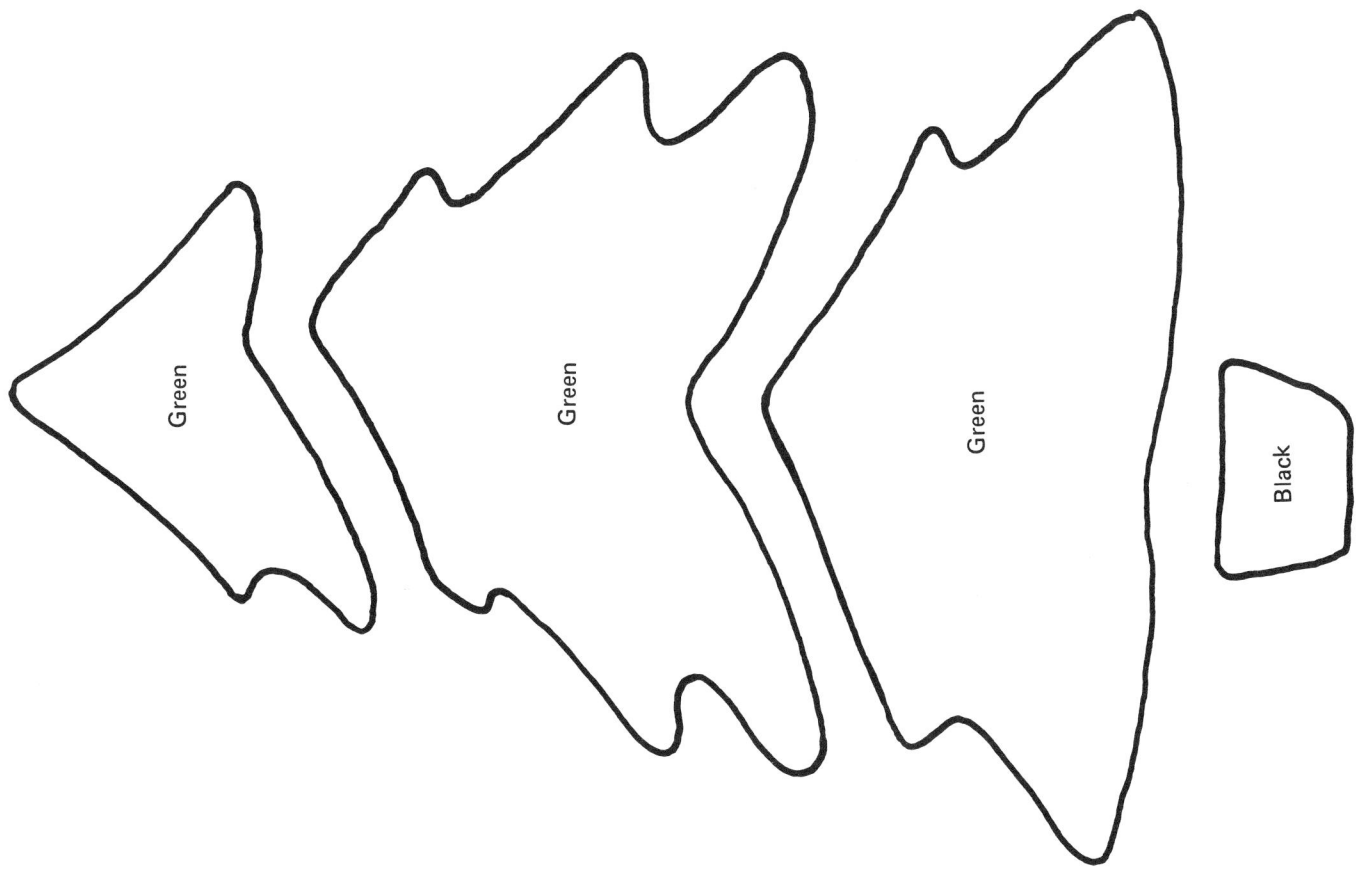

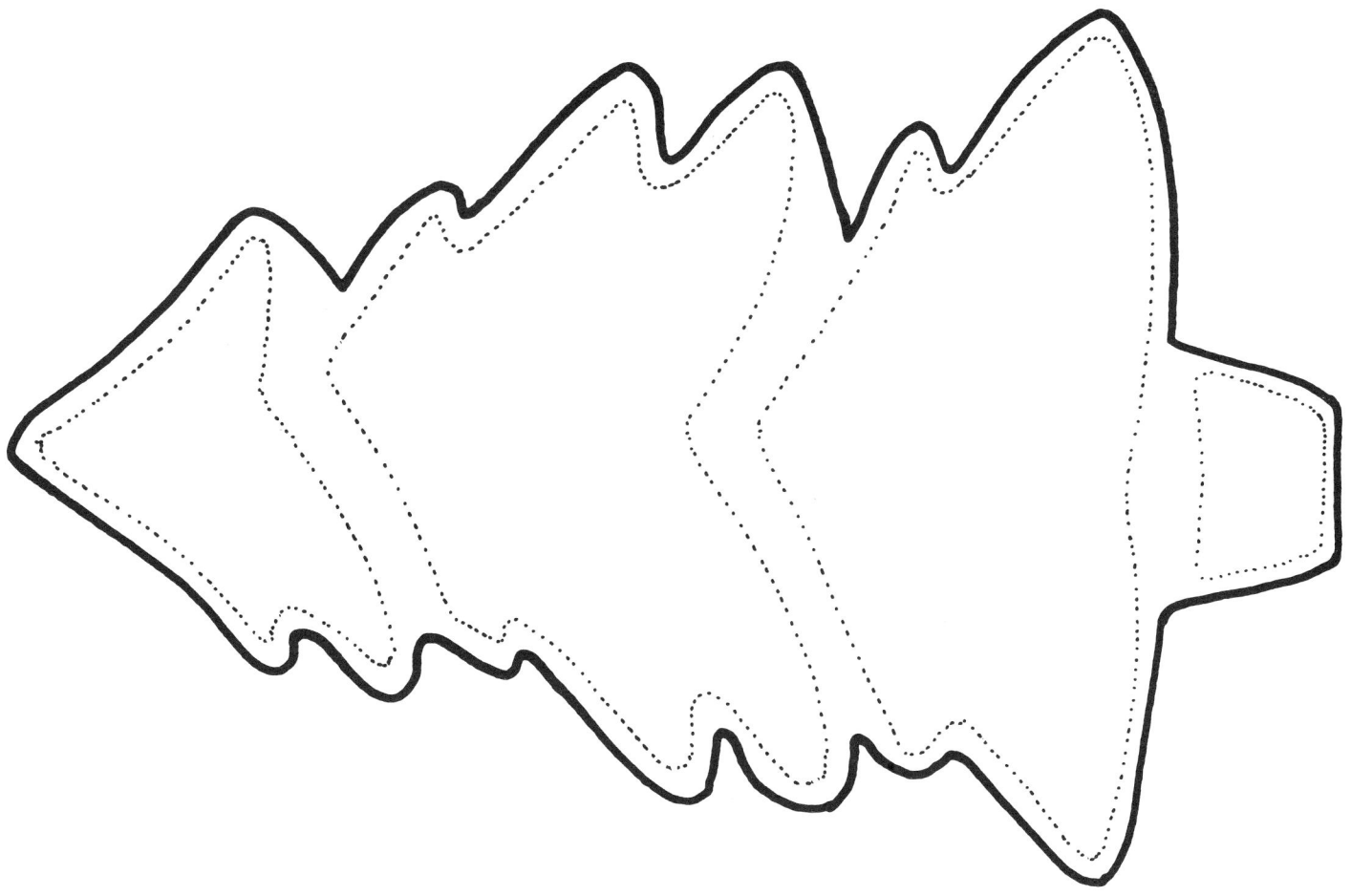

Green

Green

Green

Black

SANTA

 Black

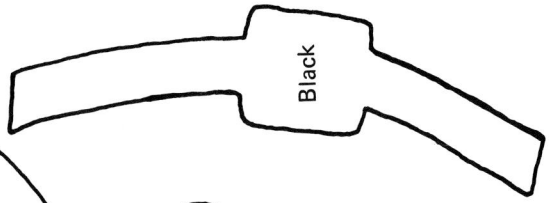 Black

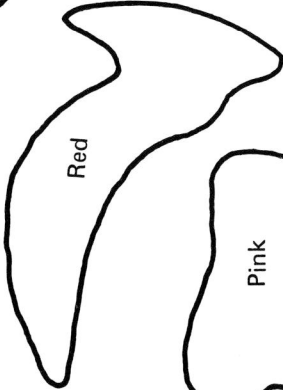 Red

Red

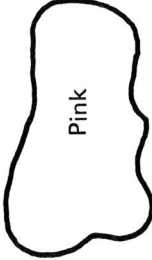 Pink

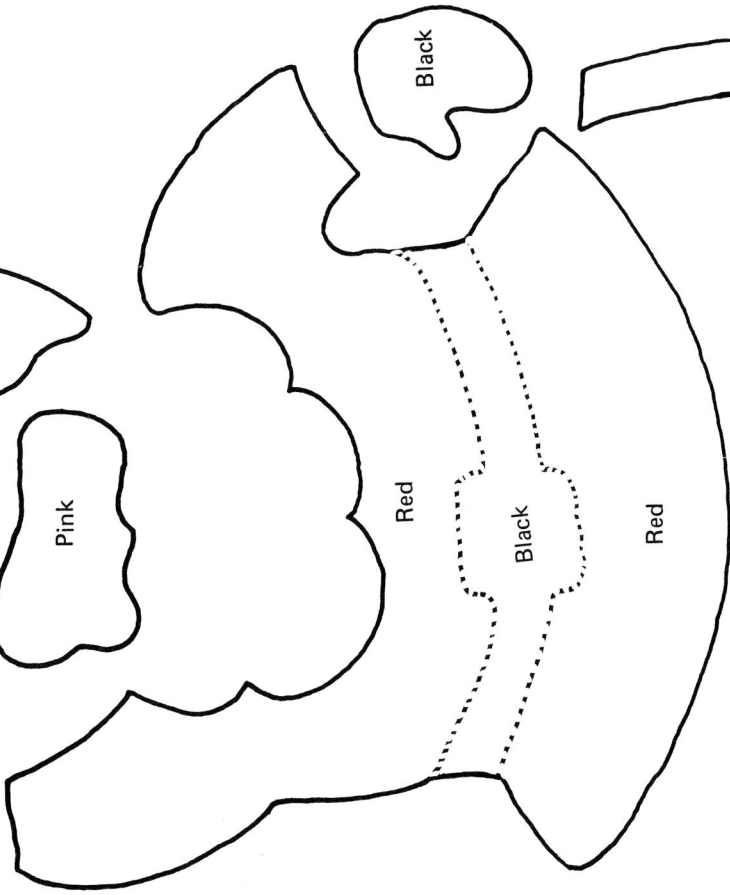 Red

Black

Red

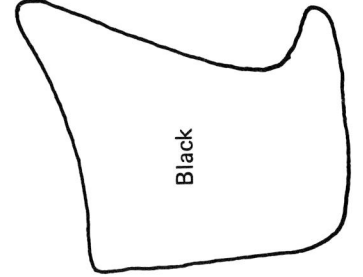 Black

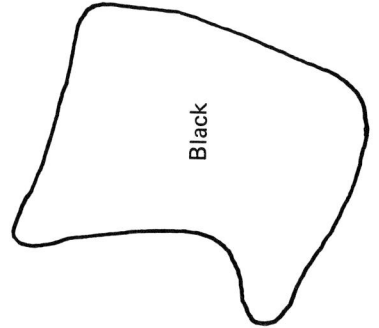 Black

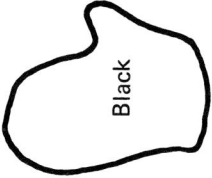 Black

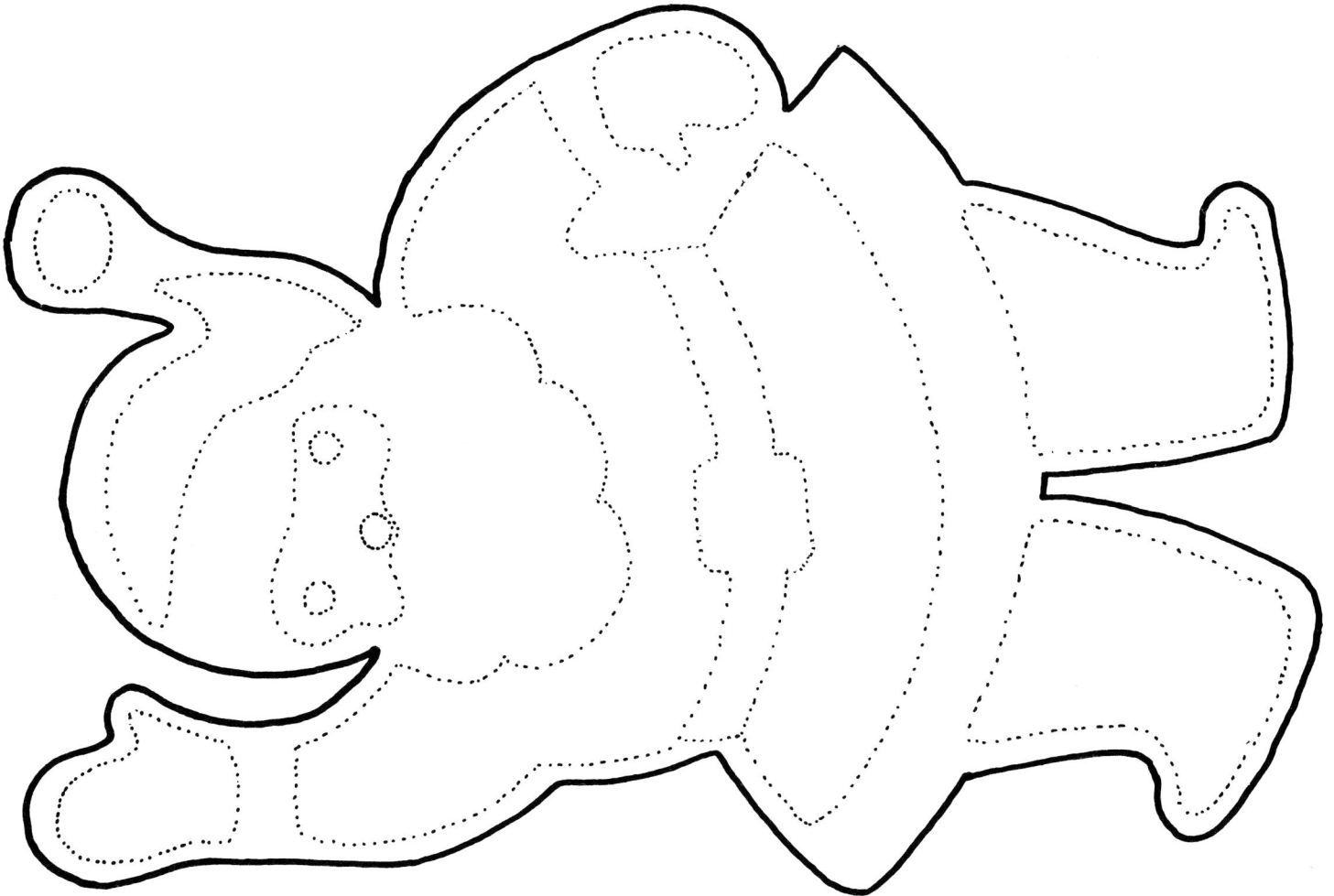

BURLAP WALLHANGING
Directions on page 34

See Diagrams for placement of
pom-poms and felt pieces

Dark Green

Hot Pink

LEAF FOR CANDLE

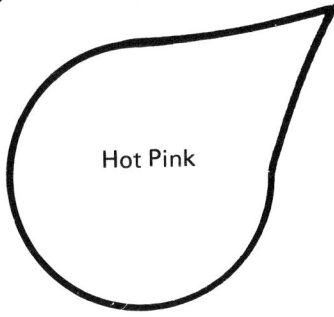

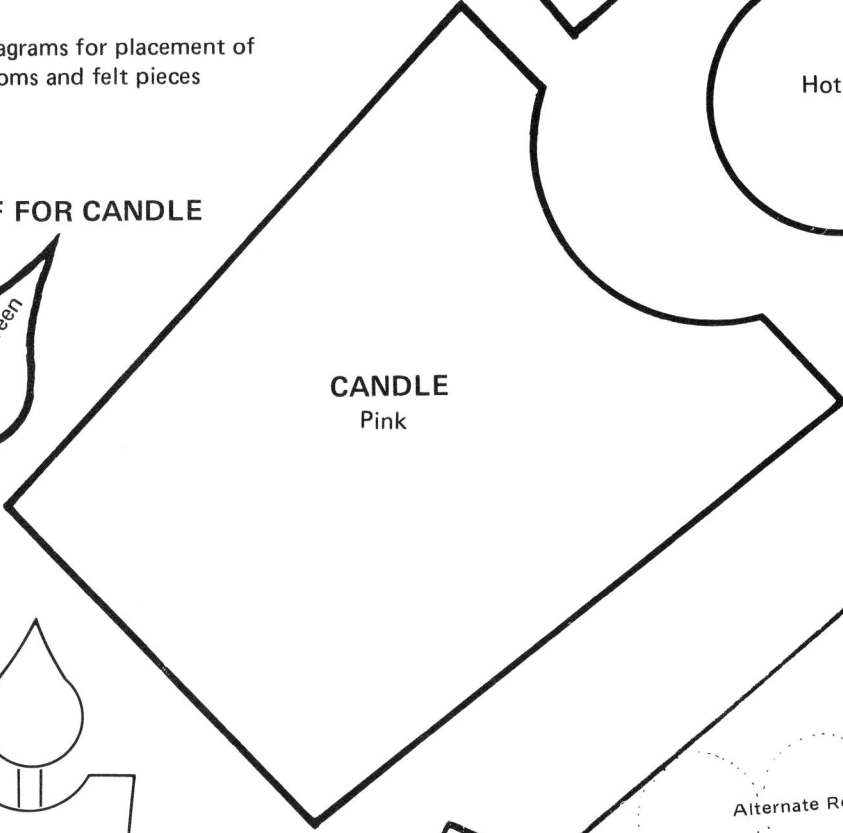

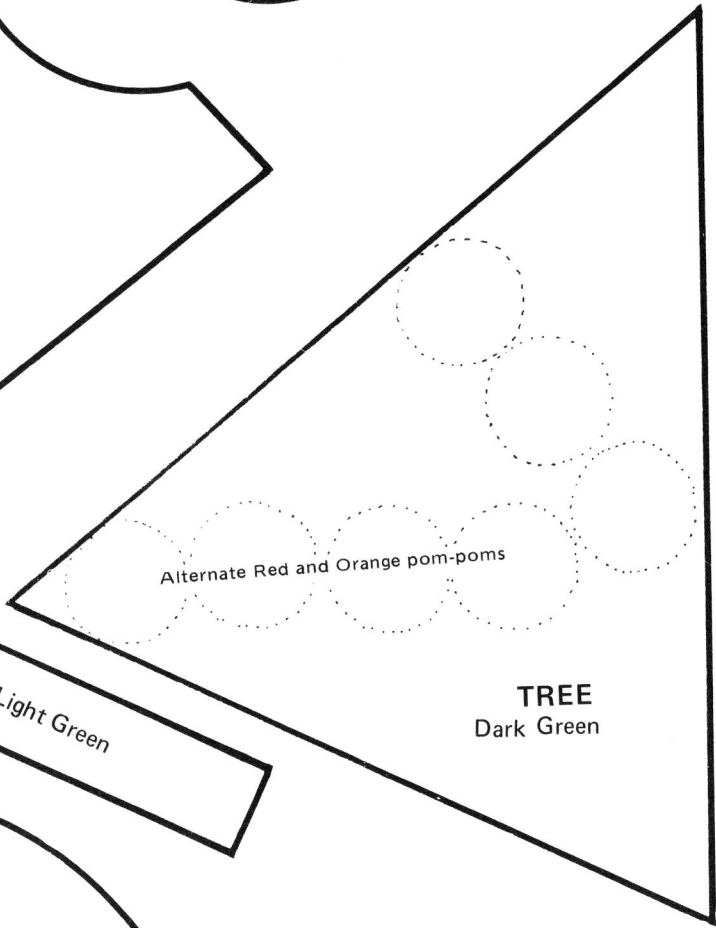

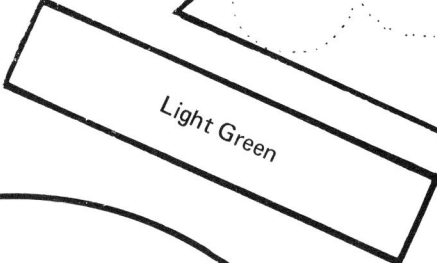

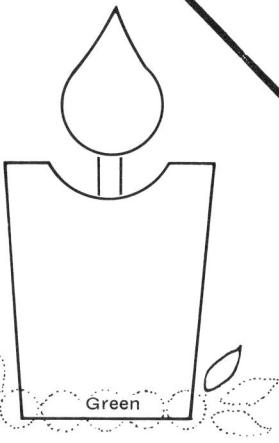

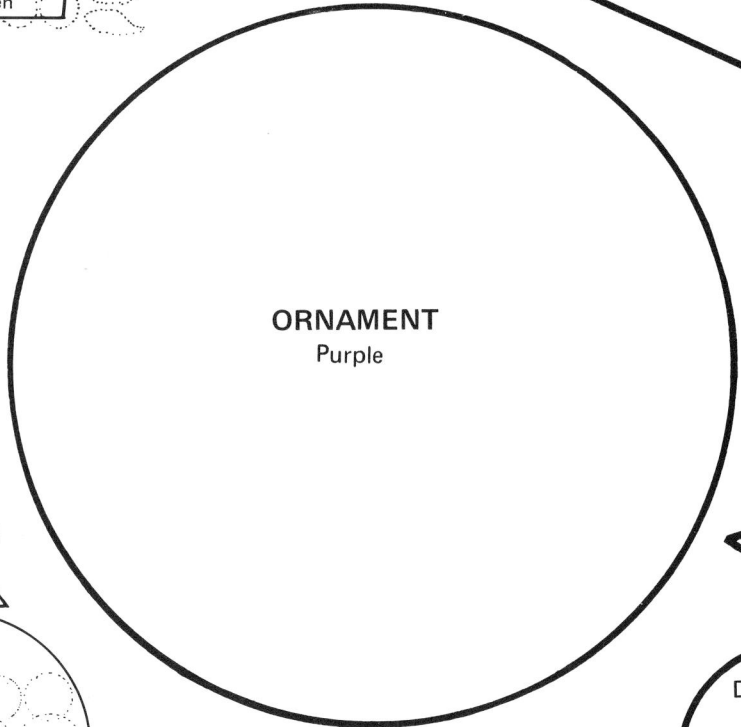

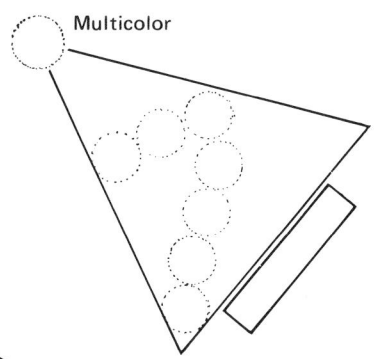

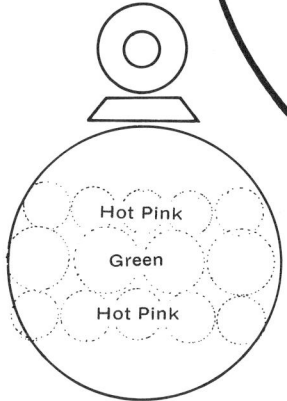

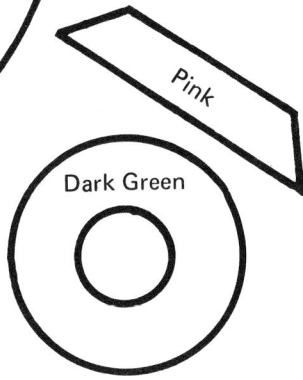

Cut 6 Dark Green

CANDLE
Pink

Green

TREE
Dark Green

Alternate Red and Orange pom-poms

Light Green

Multicolor

ORNAMENT
Purple

Hot Pink

Green

Hot Pink

Pink

Dark Green

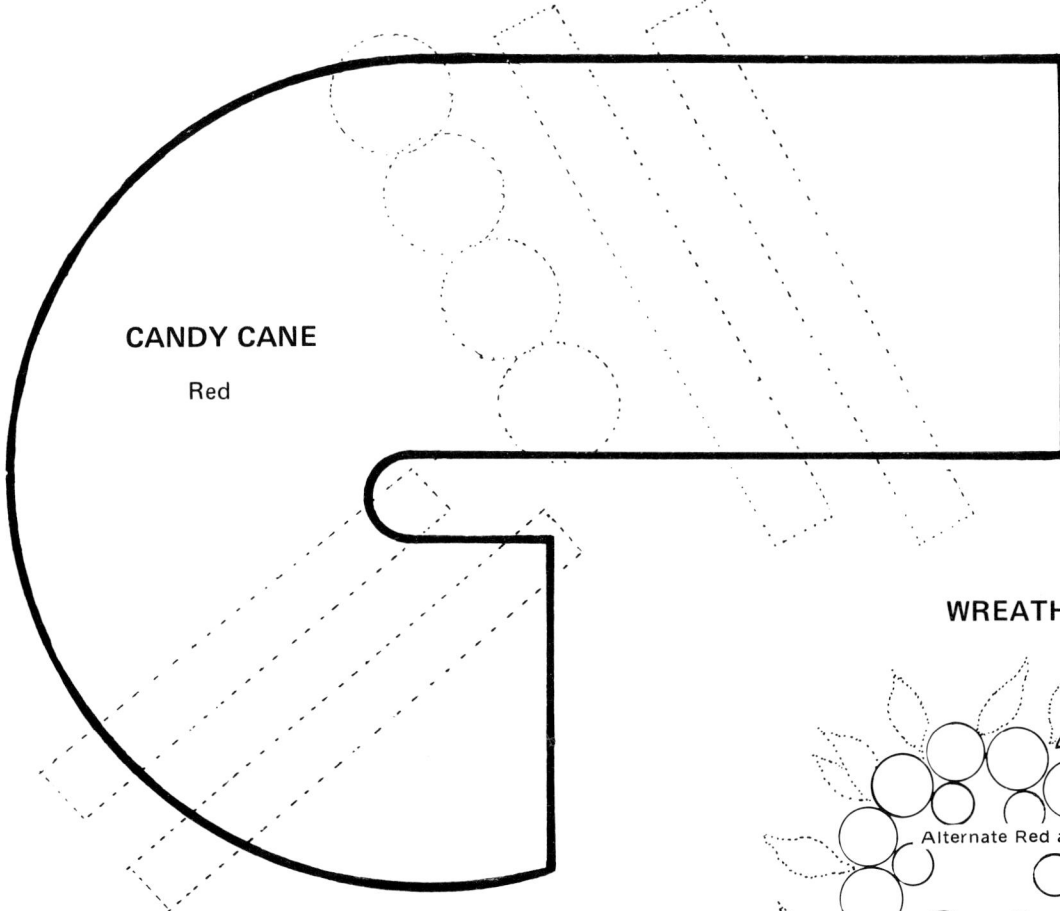

CANDY CANE

Red

Cut 4 Pink

WREATH

Alternate Red and Multicolor pom-poms

LEAF FOR WREATH

Cut 7 Light Green

Cut 8 Dark Green

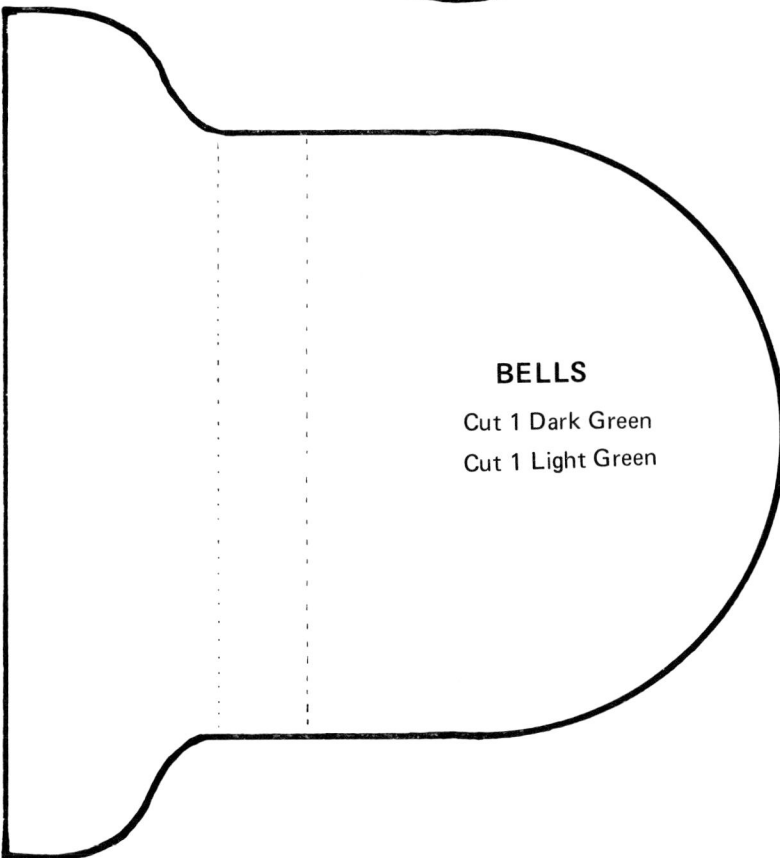

BELLS

Cut 1 Dark Green

Cut 1 Light Green

Cut 2 Pink

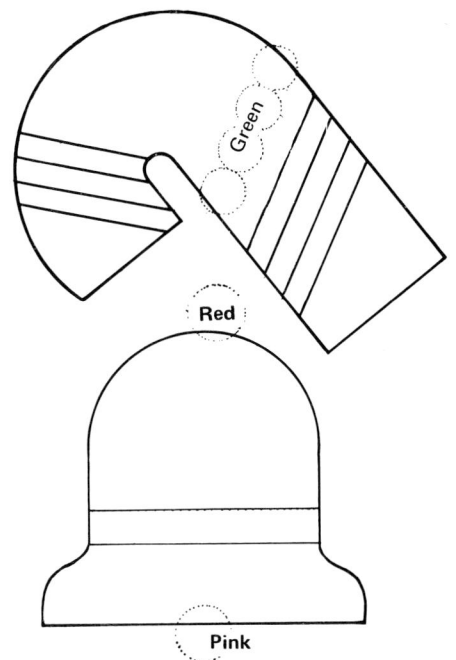

Green

Red

Pink

Fold

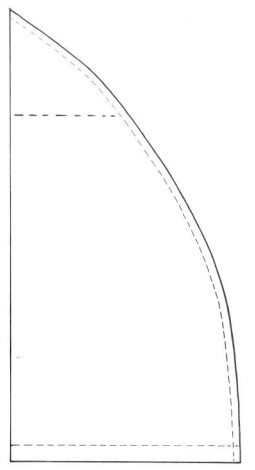

Cut After Unfolding Pattern

Trace pattern on paper with enough folded over at top fold to trace tip of cap (see diagram). Use your paper pattern on fabric.

MOP SANTA
Directions on page 34

Place on Fold

Seam Line

Red

Tack Top of Cap Here

1/2-in. Hem

103

2" 3"

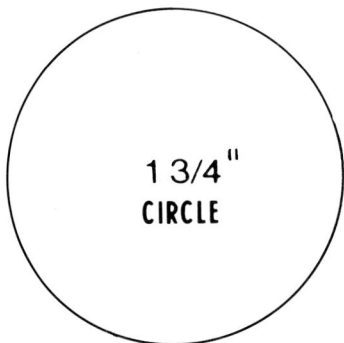

1 3/4"
CIRCLE

3/4"
CIRCLE

PATTERN FOR
CHRISTMAS COOKIE TREE

Directions on page 48
Photo on page 46

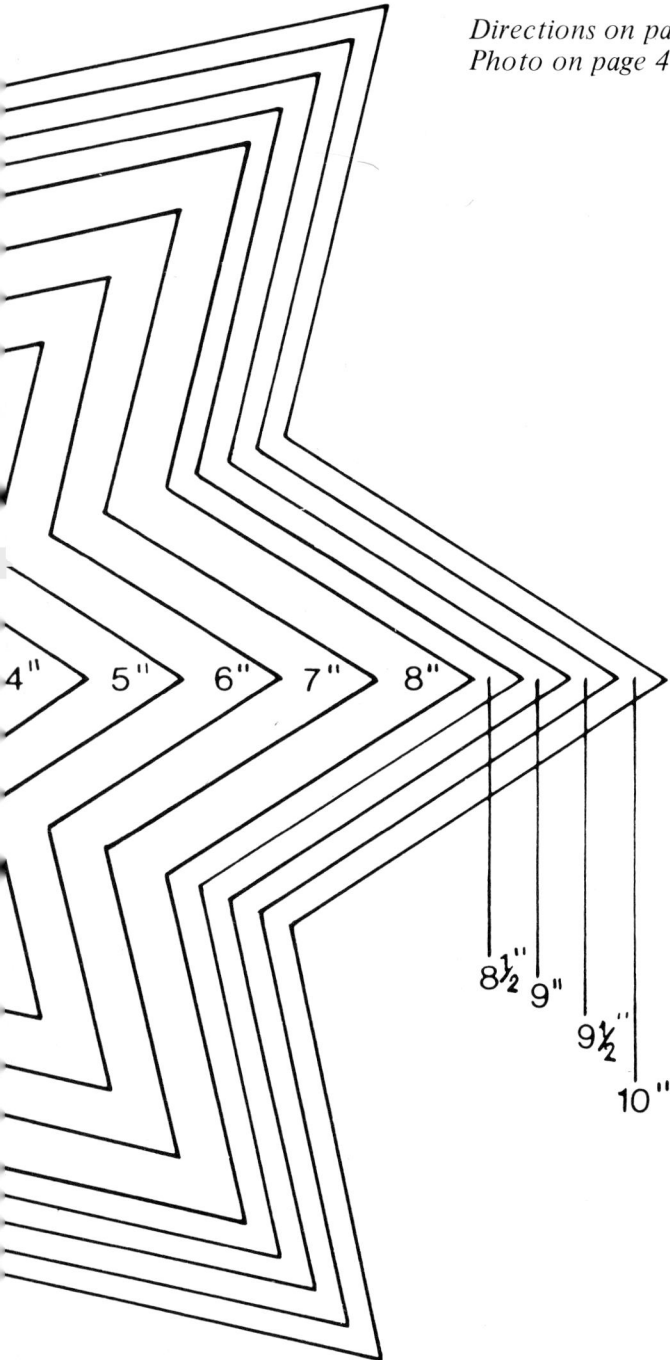

4" 5" 6" 7" 8"

8½" 9"

9½"

10"